CYBERSPEAK

An Online Dictionary

ANDY IHNATKO

Random House
New York

Cyberspeak: An Online Dictionary

Copyright © 1997 by Random House, Inc.

Published in the United States by Random House, Inc., New York and simultaneously in Canada by Random House of Canada, Limited.

"Random House" and colophon are trademarks of Random House, Inc.

Library of Congress Cataloging-in-Publication Data
Ihnatko, Andy.
     Cyberspeak : an online dictionary / Andy Ihnatko. — 1st ed.
              p.   cm.
     ISBN 0-679-77095-X (pbk.)
    1. Internet (Computer network) — Dictionaries. 2. Online information services — Dictionaries. 3. Computers — Dictionaries.
I. Title.
TK5105.875.I57I36   1997
004.6'03 — dc20   96-42055
                                                  CIP

Typeset and printed in the United States of America

Cover Design: Elektrik Grafitti, New York

Interior Book Design and Page Composition: The Book Forge, New York

ISBN 0-679-77095-X
First Edition
0 9 8 7 6 5 4 3 2 1

Random House
New York Toronto London Sydney Auckland

Foreword

First off, I do hope that you all understand the true nature of language and its role in human society. The whole concept of a new language for each new physical or social region came about specifically so that when one Jø'hänti villager brought a visiting Iolan to meet a fellow Jø'hänti, he could smile and say "Ici wäntori ven Iolan. My Iläh'o insict illä mohärbäthänti" instead of "See this Iolan here? I think his rib cage will make a good replacement for that lobster trap you lost last week."

This, and the fact that in almost every language the roots of the word for "foreigner" mean "those uncouth heathens over yonder," should bring home the point that the true purpose of language is to reenforce the divisions between society's tribes, or at least to make things difficult enough to understand so that the riff-raff keeps out. The new language of the Internet, spoken by a great number of rather insular types who like to keep interpersonal contact to a bare minimum to begin with, is no exception. After all, I mean, this whole Internet thing is a fairly cushy racket for hardcore netgeeks like yours truly. With basic understanding of the Internet, the tools for accessing it and the machinery which makes it work, we have been able to set ourselves up in cushy, exotic lifestyles involving wearing tee shirts and sweatpants all day, watching *Mystery Science Theater 3000* while lunching on ramen noodles and Dr. Pepper, and occasionally doing a little consulting work at $300 an hour. It's quite a racket, and you can understand our view that the fewer people able to talk about how the thing works, the better.

So why, then, have I turned against my geekish brethren? First, because publishing is an even cushier racket than Internet consulting, and second, because my tenth reunion is coming up. When trapped in a conversation with a former classmate in which photos of children and the phrase "The first million is always the hardest" play prominently, I would rather counter with something juicy like "Oh, I've just finished writing a dictionary for Random House" instead of falling back on the story about the time last year when I found two prizes in a box of Froot Loops.

And so, I have accepted this Dictionary-writing mandate: to allow you to understand the stuff you read and hear and get by without having to rely on extreme hand gestures reminiscent of American tourists trying to ask a French hotel clerk where the beach is. The accent is on practical terms and slang, stuff you're actually likely to come across, rather than the "kewl" terminology like "j00IYTemaSK." j00IYTemaSK, if you're curious, means "that black space between the image on your monitor and the physical edge of the screen," and appears to have been invented by a junior-high schooler in Weston, Massachusetts and only used once thereafter. The lingo you'll find here is all in common currency, I assure you, and you'll find none of the faux-hip-sterisms which would only have marked you as a hapless wannabe. I've also skipped over the mountains of slang which, while absolutely authentic, aren't in common use outside of a few specific research labs. For that sort of exhaustive examination of geek speak, I urge you to plug http://www.ccil.org/jargon/jargon.html into your browser to access The Jargon File, which is the net community's communal attempt to get every single bit of geekish jargon into some canonical form. Even if you don't care what they used to call the microwave ovens at SAIL, it's a dashed entertaining (and enormous) overview of geek history and culture. There's also heavy attention to technical terms, which are, of course, more highly valued by the Internet community as commodities for confusing outsiders.

Actually, that reminds me of another thing I wanted to warn you about. Here and there, you might be frustrated by the fact that I've called your attention to a valuable piece of freeware, for example, but forgot to give you a URL where you can get the thing. Well, that's intentional. There's a curse, a curse so potent and vile that writers dare not give it a name, which guarantees that as soon as you include a reference to a time-honored resource in your book, that resource vanishes. No kidding. My first book was on Macintosh telecommunications, and I delighted in listing glowing reviews of my favorite BBS's, complete with phone numbers. Each board had been in constant operation for upwards of a decade, but none could survive *The Curse:* in the months between completion of the manuscript and its actual publication, every one of 'em went under.

Oh, sure, I can tell you that my own website, Andy Ihnatko's Colossal Waste Of Bandwidth can be found at http://www.zdnet.com/~macuser/people/andyi/; the risk is mine to take. But dangit, I care far too much about John Norstad's megaginchy Macintosh newsreader NewsWatcher to callously throw its future into jeopardy. And besides, thanks to the very nature of the Web, individual URLs are unimportant; by accessing any online search engine (look here under "Search Engine" for a list of URLs), plugging in the very name of a product or concept will result in at least a dozen different URLs pointing to the same resource.

A final word: BLEFF. Thank you and good night.

~ Online Jargon *Noun/Adjective*

···

See *Instead:* **tilde**

^ Online Style

···

Precedes a character to symbolize a Control
sequence. "Type ^C" therefore means to hold down
the Control key and then hit "C."

. Online Jargon *Noun/Verb*

···

In DOS, a wildcard which means "all files." It's slipped
into the parlance to refer to "everything" or "all of the
members in this set," as in "Hey, be sure to invite *.*
to the wrap party, OK?" Pronounced "star-dot-star."

_ Online Style

···

The ASCII equivalent of italics. Typing in all caps is
SHOUTING, but surrounding a word with underscores
means your just want to add a _little_ emphasis.

> Online Style

···

The most common symbol that introduces parts of a
reply that are quoted from the message you're reply-
ing to. New ones get stuck in front of old ones, indi-

cating replies to replies, and replies to replies to
replies, etc.

Example | >> He was arrested for jumping into
a fountain and imitating a duck.

> Why a duck?

Oh, _do_ shut up.

ACK   Online Jargon   *Noun*

The low-level signal comm equipment sends to another piece of equipment to acknowledge that a packet
of information was received properly. Used colloquially
in a conversation to mean "You've stated your case
quite plainly forty times over; please stop talking
before one of us dies." Also as a general "Hi, I'm here."
See Also: **NAK**

Acrobat   Technical Term   *Noun*

Adobe's platform-independent file format for documents. Normally, when you try to open a word-
processed document which a friend's sent you, you
run into a bunch of problems: first, you need to own
the same word processor which your pal used to create the document, and if you don't have the same
fonts installed in your computer, some odd looking
substitutions will be made. And then you find that he
forgot to include some of the graphics files. An
Acrobat file can be read by any computer which has a

free copy of Acrobat Reader installed. All formatting will be intact, and, if fonts are missing, it'll create a brand-new font which preserves the formatting. Acrobat files have names which end with .PDF (short for Portable Document File). .PDF files are very popular on the Net because it allows a writer to create a complicated document that everybody can read no matter which software or computer system they own. Adobe also has written a plug-in for popular browsers that allow .PDF files to be displayed as part of a webpage's content.

admin   Technical Term   *Noun*

General term referring to whichever administrator is in charge of whatever online entity you happen to be talking about, such as the manager of a mailing list, honcho of a message forum, or just the pencil pusher at your company who hands out the e-mail accounts ("Tell the admin to pull Ed's account; he's been sending disparaging e-mail to Lyle Lovett again.")

-age   Online Jargon   *Suffix/Modifier*

Can be applied to the end of nearly any word to give it a larger or broader meaning. A key to translation of <word>age is to plug the word into the form "Various <word>-related stuff," as in "Hey, lay in some foodage," or "I've spend the last hour weeding all the nettage out." Often it's just a stylistic flourish without any meaning. Much like any Barbra Streisand movie.

agent   Technical Term   *Noun*

A piece of software which reaches out into the Internet or your computer and does something on your behalf. For instance, many commercial word processors come with built-in "agents," so addressing an envelope means just providing the "agent" with the right addresses…the agent controls the word processor, typing the info in and formatting it properly. One of the most popular pie-in-the-sky ideas are those of Internet Agents. Over time, this piece of software on your machine learns that you like to know the latest Red Sox scores, that you always read newspaper items about Massachusetts politics, have invested money in LambadaWare, etc. And so every morning, the program will go out on the Internet searching for any new information it thinks you might be interested in.

.aif   Technical Term   *Noun*

File extension for AIFF-format soundfiles.

AIX   Product   *Noun*

IBM's own flavor of UNIX.

alpha   Technical Term   *Noun*

Description of an early stage in the status of a project, usually a piece of software which is being developed. If it's "in alpha," then a working version of the software has been completed, though it's still far from completely tested and features may still be added or removed before it's officially released. *See Also:* **beta, gold**

alpha test   Technical Term   *Noun/Verb*

Preliminary testing of a piece of software which is in a very early stage of development. Typically, an "alpha test" doesn't go outside the boundaries of the software company's offices.

alt   Online Entity   *Noun*

See Instead: **newsgroup**

AltaVista   Online Entity   *Noun*

Exhaustive Internet search engine run by Digital, found at http://www.altavista.digital.com/. It's huge and wickedly fast.

America Online   Online Entity   *Noun*

Aka AOL, it's the most popular commercial online service, at least in terms of number of people who've signed up for the thing. America Online's marketing is so pervasive that you can't buy a bottle of salad dressing without finding a free America Online sign-up disk

attached, along with an offer of ten free hours of
usage. Because of this, many people (OK, mostly AOL's
competitors) would like to suggest that if AOL were
to weed its user database of people whose usage of
AOL lasted about as long as the salad dressing, AOL's
official census of users would be cut in half. Why sign
up with America Online? It's by far the most painless
and friendly introduction to the Online Universe. The
entire service is navigated through big, fat, colorful buttons, and everything you can do is rather neatly laid
out in front of you. For this reason, AOL seems to be
the service of choice for trendy outfits like MTV and
"The Oprah Winfrey Show" when they want to establish an online presence. Also, unlike CompuServe (CIS)
and the Internet Proper, it's very, very easy for brand-
new users to find something interesting within minutes
of their first sign-on. With the Internet Proper and CIS
to a lesser extent, new users will strike gold only after
they spend a certain amount of time learning the layout of the place. Why avoid America Online? Well, it's
like a shopping mall. Almost every complaint about
AOL stems from this one simile. For one, it's the most
annoyingly commercial online service on this planet;
often, you'll sign on and be forced to view full-screen
advertisements, one after the other, each of which
must be individually and explicitly dismissed before
you're allowed into the service. For another, much like
a mall, it's a noisy place and often filled with smelly and
obnoxious louts who you just have to walk away from.
Public discourse tends not to get quite as deep or
engaging as it gets on CompuServe. And the administrators are fighting an agressive but losing and often
comical battle against the unseemlier element. To

stamp out AOL smut, they once banned the use of the word "breast" in any form. This of course immediately made it impossible for various online breast cancer informational and support groups to exist, while the aforementioned element continued to swap their dirty pictures unabated. Perhaps most telling is the common practice of women assuming nongender-specific screen names, to avoid what one user referred to me as "inevitable and unrelenting" invitations into sex-chat rooms. Finally, as a minor point, special America Online client software is required to access the service. For most users, this isn't a hang-up at all, but it does mean that if you happen to be using a machine that can't run the client (like if you're on a business trip with your old notebook computer), you won't be able to get your e-mail. Just IMHO, of course, AOL is a fine entree into the Internet, but eventually it'll be time to take the training wheels off and move to CIS or a proper Internet connection.

analog   Online Jargon   *Adjective*

In technical terms, an analog signal is one that is not a simple sequence of "ons" and "offs" (like a stream of data). In the parlance, it has several meanings. It's used to refer to anything in the Real World as opposed to online (e.g., "my digital address is andyi@world.std.com; my analog address is P.O. Box 852, Norwood, MA 02062"). It also popularly refers to any thing or concept that cannot be readily explained or understood ("God is analog; the Devil is digital"), or something which is sloppy and inefficient ("I don't read newspapers; they're just too analog for me"). *See Also:* **digital**

ANSI   Technical Term   *Noun*

American National Standards Institute. The organization which creates or certifies all of the standards under which this great nation operates and fluorishes. Also a standard terminal type popular with DOS-based terminal programs.

ANSI graphics   Technical Term   *Noun*

A somewhat antique term. Way back in the Eighties, before many of you kids were even born, it came to pass that a standard "extended" set of ASCII text was created. Part of this set were little graphic doo-dads (card suits, musical notes, happy faces, and little line segments), which meant that for the first time in creation, it became possible to log onto a bulletin board and see text surrounded by a rectangle. You kids today, ya growed up spoiled with your Web and your cu-cme and whatnot. This was hot stuff back then. Back then, "supports ANSI graphics" was a big deal, but of course its day is long gone.

ANSI music   Technical Term   *Noun*

A historic, historic moment in the grand pageant of online communications. Simply put, it was a simple standard a BBS could use to tell your computer's ter-

minal program to chirp a specific note. You could be
signed on and wanting to just get your mail and log
right off, but you had to wait for the complete version
of the "Monty Python's Flying Circus" theme to spill
out before the BBS would allow you to continue. It is
therefore historic in that it's the first technology that
allowed the manager of an online entity to frustrate
the bejeezus out of the users by throwing in a time-
wasting bit of fluff just because he thought it was cool.
Fourteen years before the World Wide Web! Amazing!

answerbot   Technical Term   *Noun*

Software that is set up specifically to field incoming
requests via e-mail and mail back predetermined
responses. For instance, the administrator of a discussion list might leave an answerbot running so that if
someone sends e-mail with a predefined command in
the subject line ("SEND ME INFO") a text file
explaining the discussion list and how to join it will
immediately be sent back as a reply.

antivirus   Online Jargon   *Noun*

A program designed to search for viruses on your
computer and squash 'em, and/or prevent viruses
from infecting your machine in the first place.

AOL   Online Entity   *Noun*

See *Instead:* **America Online**

API Technical Term *Noun*

Application Program Interface. A formal description of all of the low-level hooks and subroutines of a piece of software, which allows another piece of software to expoit its features. Usually, an API adds features to a larger piece of software, such as an operating system. WinSock, for instance, is an API which adds TCP features to Microsoft Windows.

app Online Jargon *Noun*

Application; a slick program for end-users (like a word processor or a spreadsheet) as opposed to system-level software. In the past decade, a need developed for a term which referred to the sort of software which end-users used, and not the stuff which the programmers, administrators, and hackers pounded on. In the olden days, way back when "M*A*S*H" was on TV, you understand, software was software because almost everyone who used a word processor was also proficient with the operating system itself and probably could even write software if s/he wanted or needed to. But time marches on, and we now need a specialized term so that we don't have to answer confused e-mail asking why nothing happened when they tried to "run" that font file they downloaded earlier.

Apple Company *Noun*

Makers of Macintosh computers and the Macintosh operating system, and ironclad evidence of the existance of God. I mean, someone's looking out for Apple's corporate well-being, and it sure isn't Apple. While Microsoft was making sound business decisions like forcing the Pope to sign an agreement to pay Microsoft a $50 Windows site-license fee for every copy of the Catechism in circulation, Apple was busy trying to figure out how to manufacture the first banana-shaped computer. "Invent it all and let the marketplace sort it out" was long a catchphrase at Apple, to the extreme of having a sandwich named that in the company cafeteria.

Traditionally, Microsoft wins the market-share battle rather definitively, and Apple wins the innovation battle equally definitively. Windows owners get the security of knowing that they're using the most prevalent desktop operating system, while Mac owners get to use features Windows users won't see for years.

applet   Technical Term   *Noun*

....

(1) A compiled Java program which can be run in a Java-compliant browser.

(2) A relatively small application, especially one which is run from within another application. The spreadsheet that the CFO of Random House used to figure out that this book was a good idea—that's an application. The calculator program that I used to figure out how many entries I needed to write every day to make my deadline—that's an applet.

AppleTalk   Technical Term   *Noun*

....

See *Instead:* **LocalTalk**

arc   Online Jargon   *Noun/Verb*

Short for archive. Also used as a verb, as in "I arced all of the code libraries and netted them over to you this morning."

Archie   Technical Term   *Noun*

A system of Internet servers and protocols for searching for files on FTP sites on the Net. By running an Archie client on your machine and specifying the filename you're hunting for, Archie will return a list of FTP sites in the Net that contain that file. More or less obsoleted by the explosion of the Web. Archie, after all, will only find the specific files you specify; Web search engines (like AltaVista) can find files based solely on some vague definition of the sort of thing you're interested in. *See Also:* **Veronica**

archiver   Technical Term   *Noun*

A utility which prepares files or groups of files for convenient storage or transmission. An archiver compresses files, applying algorithms which look for more efficient ways of representing the file's data (a process conceptually similar to writing "A dozen eggs" intead of "an egg an egg an egg an egg an egg an egg…") and can also combine several files into one archive file. When processed by the proper archiving program, an archived file is transmogrified back into its original state. Some archives are self-extracting; the archive file actually contains all of the machinery required for extracting its own contents. So instead of running a separate utility, you can just run the archive itself. Archiving is a good thing, especially for online stuff. First, it means that instead of taking up 200K of space, that cool shareware game can be turned into a 50K archive file, which means that it'll only take a quarter of the time to download. Second, the fact that the game and all of its related files have been smooshed together into a single unit means that you won't have to track down all of the separate bits of the game (like the game itself, the documentation, the sound and graphics files, etc.) and download each separately.

ARPAnet   Technical Term   *Noun*

The larval stage of the Internet. This whole mess began in 1969 as four colleges were doing research for the government and needed to share data and hardware. So their computers got wired together and, bang, forty years later you can launch Netscape and see a live picture of someone's parrot in Portland. Got its name from the Advanced Research Projects Agency, which funded the thing at the beginning. Phun Phact: the total lack of any sort of centralized computer that manages the network is an outgrowth of the Cold War mentality: if nukes wiped out any part of the country, The Gummint wanted to be sure that the other part could send and receive e-mail. Hence, holistic interdependence.

ASCII   Technical Term   *Noun*

(1) Technically speaking, the American Standard Code for Information Interchange. A standard system for

encoding letters of the alphabet, digits, and symbols supported by every computer on the planet, which ensures that when you type the letter "A" on your keyboard and transmit it, it'll appear as an "A" at the other end of the connection and not as a "&." A less widely accepted standard is "high ASCII," which is for all of those specialty characters (such as ™, £, and ~) that weren't included when the ASCII system was first defined. If someone sends you a message containing bizarre characters where quotes should be, it's likely that their computer uses different codes for "curly quotes" than yours does.

(2) A standard file format consisting of nothing but ASCII text. No fancy formatting or font information is included in the file, but the file can be read by any computer anywhere.

ASCII Art   Online Jargon   *Noun*

Artwork made up entirely of low-ASCII characters. It runs the gamut from simple little doo-dads in some-one's sigfile to complicated random-dot 3D stere-ogram images which really work. The patron saint of ASCII art is probably the humble but proud cow, depicted thousands of times in a thousand different situations. This one's not doing anything at all:

But just like elephant jokes and banjo jokes, everyone has to get into the act and show us what this cow would look like if he were surprised, or going trick-or-treating dressed as Bill Gates, or surfing, etc. *See Also:* **emoticons**

ASCII-bashing   Online Jargon   *Noun*

Jiggering around the format of the information in a text file, not the information itself. For instance, you're now looking at the product of text-bashing; this book was written in a database with fields for all the different parts of the definition, and then exported into a text file. Once the final design went gold, some ASCII-bashing was done to the file to put all of the fields in an order that the page-layout software could fit into the layout.

ASCII-gram   Style

See Instead: **emoticons**

asynchronous   Technical Term   *Noun*

Technically a term referring to the nuts-and-bolts nature of a comm connection, basically saying that the machine at either end can send data to the other whenever it wants to without waiting for "stop" bits to clear. Almost all of your telecommunications are asynchronous. In parlance, this is often applied to people. "Jim's in asynchronous mode," you might say, of a per-

son who talks and talks and talks without letting anyone else get a word in edgeways.

AT Command Set   Technical Term   *Noun*

The Esperanto of modems, except that the AT Set
really is the language supported by absolutely everyone, allowing hardware from disparate origins to embrace and work together harmoniously. Your comm
software operates your modem by sending it commands,
all of which begin with AT (short for "Attention!"). For
instance, to dial the number 555-1212, your software
sends the command "ATDT 555-1212." AT tells the
modem that what follows is a command, D means
dial, T means use touch-tone, and the rest you know.
Your modem probably arrived with a reference card
listing all of its AT commands, or maybe they're silk-
screened on its case or burned into the modem's
memory as a help file. It's important to keep these
commands handy. Normally, you'll never need to man-
ually enter any sort of modem command, but if you
ever find yourself in a hotel room needing to get your
e-mail, but finding that your notebook's modem balks
at the hotel phone system's oddball dial tone, you'll be
grateful that you were able to enter a command to
order the modem not to wait for a dial tone.

AT&T chipset   Technical Term   *Noun*

Modem firmware designed and manufactured by
AT&T. Often used as a loose synonym for "This
modem can be used with a cellular phone."

ATM   Technical Term   *Noun*

....

(1) Asynchronous Transfer Mode. A low-level communications protocol that is getting a lot of press because
it works well with all kinds of data and all kinds of different installations. For those reasons, magazine articles
that talk about cable companies serving movies over
the Internet often feature this buzzword prominently;
ATM is practically synonymous with those "your voice
line is also your modem line, your cable hook-up, and
your IV Ringers drip" schemes.

(2) Not to be confused with Adobe Type Manager, the
Adobe system extension for Mac and Windows which
allows these systems to display PostScript fonts
onscreen as normal display fonts.

attachment   Technical Term   *Noun*

....

A file that is digitally "enclosed" inside a mail message.
Your mailreader program will automatically process
this file and give you the option of saving it to disk. *See
Also:* **MIME**

atto-   Online Jargon   *Suffix/Modifier*

....

Prefix meaning ten to the power of negative eighteen.
Therefore used to diminufy something to the ultimate
degree:

Example ```
I will devote nine attointerest
units to your proposal.
```
```

.au   Technical Term   *Noun*

File extension for Apple/Sun "Sound" file format.

AUP   Online Jargon   *Noun*

Acceptible Use Policy. Your ISP's written policy concerning how you may use its services. For instance, your company's AUP might demand that you use their T3 connection to send status reports to the main office and not to download 5M QuickTime movies of "Baywatch" babes.

avatar   Online Jargon   *Noun*

A collection of electrons on the Internet that represents you. Most commonly used to refer to an online entity you've defined for yourself on a MUD (hence Bill Peterson, junior analyst at Fleet Bank/Boston, goes home, jumps into his MUD and becomes Frodo Cuplighter-Wavesinger, elf in the court of Jardeela), but also a technical term used by companies developing interactive virtual reality-ish Internet services; your "avatar" is a little cartoon guy on the screen who you direct to walk through VR environments, talk to other users, etc. Sometimes also used to refer to the superuser of a system.

AVI   Technical Term   *Noun*

Microsoft Windows's file standard for digital video. An

.AVI file can nonetheless be played on Macintosh and UNIX machines by downloading the appropriate player software.

awk   Technical Term   *Noun*

UNIX utility for ASCII-bashing, taking a text file (a file of exported database data, say) and processing it so that it can be used by another program.

Baby Bell   Online Jargon   *Noun*

One of the half-dozen or so regional phone companies that resulted when The Gummint smashed up "The" phone company.

backbone   Online Jargon   *Noun*

(1) A general term meaning "that thing that everything else hangs off of." For instance, a Backbone Mail Site is one of the key sites on the Internet that processes and distributes mail to hundreds of other sites; "Our office runs on an Ethernet backbone" means that while there may be several networks and even several different kinds of networks, they all plug into a single Ethernet cable that runs throughout the entire office.

(2) That thing that MIS managers lack which leads them to just buy Wintel boxes without even considering Macs.

backdoor Online Jargon *Noun*

A deliberately created weakness in a security system. The classic image of a "backdoor" is the secret password left in a company's computer system by the consultant who designed and installed it, so that if the check bounces, whammo…he can get right in and shut things down, all the while rehearsing in his head lines like "Oh dear…you say you can't get any of your files and you have a big presentation later today? Gee, sir, I'd love to help you out, but I'm afraid that as long as your account with me is so far past due. …"

background process

Online Jargon *Noun*

Technically, refers to something your computer is working on while you, the user, are actively operating another program. It has a similar meaning conversationally, meaning a less-important task that is getting your sporatic (and disinterested) attention while you concentrate on your primary task; that is, "Don't worry…I'm working hard on that code, but unfortunately I've got my sister's kids here in the house as a background process." *See Also:* **multitask**

backslash Online Jargon *Noun*

(1) The "\" character.

(2) The "/" character, which is actually just a "slash."

(3) What is done to people who load up their web-pages with tiles, flashing text, and animated text after they've been pounded and slashed.

bagbiter   Online Jargon   *Noun*

Loser, idiot, moron; (as an adjective **backbiting**) worthless. Refers to software ("Will someone please kindly inform this bagbiting word processor that I do indeed have a printer connected to my machine?!!!") as well as people ("Cripes, the conference was great, except for this one bagbiter who kept interrupting to tell us about this Tom Servo robot he built. ...")

Bamf!   Online Jargon   *Interjection*

The final uttering of someone who's about to leave a live conference. Comes from the *X-Men* comic book, in which the character Nightcrawler makes that sound effect whenever he uses his teleportation ability. Good God, I hope you never use this in public.

bandwidth   Online Jargon   *Noun*

An entity's (a phone line, a BBS, a human brain) capacity for carrying or digesting information. If someone is "narrow bandwidth," then you must communicate largely with one-syllable words and interpretive dance. If she's "wide bandwidth," then you can plunge straight in with your theories on the action of pentadeoxyribonucleatic lattices upon the lymphatic engine without worry.

Also popular is the concept of "wasting bandwidth." Ideally, when you post something on the Internet, it's something that informs and entertains without taking up too much room. If you're just posting an hour-by-hour account of your ferret's eating habits, you're wasting bandwidth. A depressingly frank awareness of the quality of my own website's content has resulted in my naming it "Andy Ihnatko's Colossal Waste of Bandwidth." (http://www.zdnet.com/macuser/people/andyi/). As with so many endeavors (Batman movies, for instance), low expectations are the key to customer satisfaction.

bang   Online Jargon   *Noun*

An exclamation point. It gets its popularity from the APL language, which uses a whole mess of symbols in place of the more English-like names you see in C++ and elsewhere; when you heard a professor speaking of "bang-jot-dot" he was just referring to a bit of APL code and wasn't succumbing to the fumes from the carpeting epoxy.

bang on   Online Jargon   *Verb*

To subject a piece of hardware or software to abuse in the hopes of uncovering bugs or flaws. Less commonly used to mean "work very hard on."

bang path   Online Jargon   *Noun*

Electronic addresses in the old UUCP mail system, in

which every hop a message must take is separated by a bang ("!").

barney   Online Jargon   *Noun*

Gently derisive term for an Internet user whose interest is only temporary; e.g., someone whose over-all unapologetic cluelessness suggests they're seated at an Internet kiosk in a coffeeshop. Different from a newbie in that newbies become plain decent folk through time and effort; a barney is gone for good once their ten free hours of AOL time are up, or they finish their $5 cup of Zimbabwe Triple Cinnamon. *See Also:* **newbie**

bass-ackwards   Online Jargon   *Noun*

Backwards.

baud   Technical Term   *Noun*

Short for Bits Audible, it refers to the number of "events" per second taking place between the sender and the receiver. Usually the baud rate is identical to the number of bits per second, but the two terms are not, technically speaking, interchangeable. There are those who derive pathetic satisfaction from smugly telling others that spiders are not insects, and so too, do certain geeks love telling people that baud $\neq$ BPS. The only proper response is to quickly reach over and pluck one of their eyebrow hairs.

BBS   Technical Term   *Noun*

Bulletin Board System. A concept which the Internet has simultaneously endangered and blurred. In classic terms, a BBS is a computer (usually a personal computer) hooked up to a modem and running BBS software. Like a more traditional online service, the BBS contains message forums, private mail, live conferencing, and piles of software available for downloading. Unlike an online service, you're dialing directly into the machine that runs the BBS software (paying long-distance charges if it's outside your local dialing area) and only a few users can be supported simultaneously. Also, a BBS typically has only rudimentary connections to other computers, if any. In contrast to the wide, wild Internet, BBSs have an intimate, clubby atmosphere and are more of a communal meeting place than an online service per se. Just as bitter old men complain that supermarkets drove grocers, bakers, and butchers out of business, bitter twentysomethings like me complain that the Internet has caused BBSs, once the backbone of the online experience, to go the way of the passenger pigeon. *See Also:* **FidoNet**

Bell 103/Bell 212A   Technical Term   *Noun*

OK, you've seen these standards mentioned in the very fine print of a modem's specifications, and you want to know what they are, so I'll tell you: they're the standards for incredibly low-speed communications. It took you maybe 1.4 seconds to read that and that was about 1.35 seconds more than the information's worth because you'll never need to communicate at 300 bps anyway. Well, it's the standard that the modems in most of those credit-card-swipe machines at the store use, but that's it.

beta Technical Term *Noun*

Description of a later stage in the status of a project, usually a piece of software under development. A "beta" version is more complete and more stable than an "alpha," and generally means the software is ready for wide testing and its list of features has been locked in. Often, a software company will release a "beta" to the Internet in the interests of getting as much testing done as possible before releasing it commercially. *See Also:* **alpha, gold**

beta test Technical Term *Noun/Verb*

Bug-testing of a piece of software preliminary to its official release. Some beta testing is done solely among a select and secret list of trusted users, but today it's becoming stylish to offer beta copies to anyone who wants to download one, in the interests of quashing as many bugs as possible and generating a good pre-release "buzz" for the product.

bfd Online Jargon *Interjection*

Big [expletive which I'm sure will occur to you] Deal.

big room   Online Jargon   *Noun*

That enormous space you enter when you leave your house and exit when you reach your school, office, computer shop, or place of worship, if otherwise. Features the Sun, and is also where a lot of really nagging Real World stuff happens to you. Also, I understand there is crime there. Give it a miss, I say. *See Also:* **Sun, Real World**

big win   Online Jargon   *Noun*

A success achieved at least partially by accident. An example of a Big Win is when you did a half-arsed job on an important report, and then accidentally compressed it using uucompress instead of PKZIP before sending it to your boss. Your boss e-mails you the next day, saying he couldn't decompress it. He apologizes for having messed up the file and asks if a week will be sufficient for you to rewrite it.

.bin   Technical Term   *Noun*

File extension for a generic binary file, or more commonly a file encoded in the Macintosh MacBinary file format.

binary   Online Jargon   *Noun*

A binary is any downloadable file that doesn't simply contain human-readable, ASCII text. Typically it refers

to a runnable program available for downloading, but
it can also refer to pictures, sounds, or movies, among
others. Most Usenet newsgroups have subgroups
specifically for binaries; a posting in
comp.sys.mac.comm might announce that
DiscoTerminal 3.2 is now available for downloading,
but the binary— the file itself—would be found in
comp.sys.mac.comm.binaries.

BinHex   Technical Term   *Noun*

An algorithm for transmogrifying a file so that it only
contains standard ASCII-type characters, and thus can
be electronically transmitted safely. As a verb, to transmogrify a file using BinHex. Really only popular on the
Mac side of things. BinHexed files usually get a file
extension of .hqx.

bis   Technical Term   *Adjective*

French adjective meaning "modified" or "enhanced."
Usually seen at the end of the name of a communications standard to indicate that it includes all of the features of the old standard and then some.

bit   Technical Term   *Noun*

The smallest possible unit of data; an "on" or "off." Just
as Hostess Twinkies, grand pianos, and Wink Martindales
are just different arrangements of atoms, all software
and files are just arrangements and sequences of bits.

BITnet   Online Entity   *Noun*

Because It's There Network. A slow and rather limited part of the Internet which you're not likely to ever come across nowadays.

biz   Online Entity   *Noun*

See *Instead:* **newsgroup**

blew up   Online Jargon   *Verb*

Failed spectacularly.

bloatware   Online Jargon   *Noun*

Software that, with every upgrade, gets more features and gobbles up more and more system resources, but adds no functionality.

bloodware   Online Jargon   *Noun*

A form of shareware in which the author requests that instead of sending hir a monetary fee, you donate blood to the Red Cross.

.BMP   Technical Term   *Noun*

File extension for Windows Bitmap graphical file format.

bogus   Online Jargon   *Adjective*

Stupid, wrong, nonfunctional, or silly. Three boatloads of different flavors of this term are all over the Net: bogosity, bogish, bogid, bogoid, ad nauseum. *See Also:* **boson**

bookmark   Technical Term   *Noun/Verb*

A standard feature of Web browsers which lets you make a record of a webpage and its address so you can find it again easily. The "bookmark" concept became so popular that it became co-opted by many other Internet programs, especially when URLs became popular. Now, "bookmark managers," independent programs which can collect and organize the URLs of every Internet destination imaginable, are quite the rage. *See Also:* **hotlist**

boson   Online Jargon   *Noun*

Term for the subatomic particle representing the most minute quantifiable unit of bogusness. This term was once all the rage, but is starting to fade.

-bot   Online Jargon   *Suffix/Modifier*

The suffix -bot suggests an operation which is automatically carried out by software left running on an Internet server. See *Also:* **cancelbot, mailbot, answerbot**

Example | Not to worry, I've got a grungebot running which automatically strips all references to L7, Nirvana, and Hole from my incoming mail.

bounce   Online Jargon   *Verb*

Sometimes a piece of e-mail is undeliverable, usually because the recipient's address is faulty; when that happens, it's returned to the sender and is said to have been bounced. Less popularly used as a synonym for forward; "I bounced a copy of your e-mail to Jerry."

box   Online Jargon   *Noun*

A generic term for a type of computer, as in a Windows box, a pre-press box, an SGI box…not referring to a specific model but nonetheless indicating the basic kind.

BPS   Technical Term   *Noun*

Speed of transmitted data, literally the number of bits being sent or received per second. See *Also:* **baud, CPS**

brain dump   Online Jargon   *Noun/Verb*

To simply empty your brain of information without the slightest care as to style, substance, or relevance to the situation at hand or whether the person you're brain-dumping to is interested. If you ask someone "Hey, did you see anything interesting at MACWORLD Expo last week?" and they reply with a 200K report beginning with the calcified sausage and eggs he ate on the plane trip over and ending with the chicken diablo he ate for dinner on the flight back, you've just witnessed a brain dump.

browser   Technical Term   *Noun*

A specialized piece of software for accessing websites. The two most popular are Netscape and Microsoft Internet Explorer.

brute-force method   Online Jargon   *Noun*

A method of solving a problem that involves trying every possible solution until you find the one which works. Traditionally it's a programming term, but is also used to refer to Real World stuff.

Example

"I suggested that we just ask someone how to get to the convention hall from our hotel, but Jeff decided to use the brute-force method instead. It took us five hours to reach the hall three blocks away, but hey, we got to see all kinds of parts of the state that we wouldn't have ordinarily visited..."

BSD   Technical Term   *Noun*

Berkeley Software Distribution, a flavor of UNIX (referred
to as BSD Unix or more popularly Berkeley Unix).
Famous quote: "Berkeley is famous for two things: BSD
and LSD. It is difficult to see this as were co-incident."

btw   Online Jargon   *Interjection*

By The Way.

bug   Technical Term   *Noun*

A defect, in hardware, software, or just life. This term's
intention is often attributed to Admiral Grace Hopper,
inventor of COBOL, but in fact, it goes back to the
nineteenth century.

bugfix   Technical Term   *Noun*

A nonspecific term for a way to turn a buggy and
overall wonky version of a piece of hardware or
software into a less buggy and wonky one. For
instance, when DiscoWare discovers that the just-
released DiscoWriter 4.0 causes hard drives to be
reformatted whenever the "Print" command is select-
ed, the company will be considerate enough to issue
a bugfix. *See Also:* **updater, patch**

bulletproof   Online Jargon   *Noun*

Absolutely unbreakable. "We've had 200 beta-testers banging on the latest version for a month; now the code's dang-near bulletproof."

byte   Technical Term   *Noun*

One character of data, consisting of eight bits. *NB*: this term has been around for decades. Please take my word for it that every conceivable joke playing on the similarity between "byte" and "bite" has already been written, and the authors all summarily smacked in the heads.

C, C++   Technical Term   *Noun*

The most popular programming language on the face of the earth, at least for now. It's pretty likely that every single piece of software you currently own, including your computer's operating system and its firmware, was written in whole or in part in C.

C&SS   Technical Term   *Noun*

See Instead: Card and Socket Services

cache   Technical Term   *Noun*

In the broader sense, a cache is a place where your

computer stores information temporarily so that the next time it's needed it can be accessed wickedly fast. Within the scope of this book, "the cache" usually refers to the file on your hard drive where your web browser stashes the last howevermany objects it's downloaded. That way, if you access the Baywatch Appreciation Page again, your browser can just read that 80K photo of David Hasselhoff from your hard drive in five seconds instead of taking a whole minute to download it from the server again. Hey, Parents! Want to see what images your kids have been down-loading in Netscape? Click in the "Location" bar and type "about:image-cache". All the images in Netscape's cache will be displayed. Hey, Kids! Worried that your parents might have read this? Under the "Options" menu, select the "Network Preferences" item and then click the button marked "Clear Cache Now."

cancelbot   Technical Term   *Noun*

....

Software left running on an Internet server that auto-matically looks for and deletes any Usenet posting from a person (or containing a subject) which the sys-tem administrator doesn't cotton to. Cancelbots are rare things, and almost always are used to defend a site's news server from incoming spam from a notori-ous address.

canon   Online Jargon   *Noun*

....

The official and unquestionable source of information on a subject. "According to canon, Shatner used a special high-tech submersible hairpiece for that scene in *Star Trek IV: The Voyage Home*." The implication is that this is such an accepted truth that no one would even think of questioning it. In truth, it might mean that the writer has real confidence that if pressed, he could indeed find written proof to back his statement up.

Card and Socket Services
Technical Term   *Noun*

Low-level software that allows a computer to control a PC Card device.

careware   Online Jargon   *Noun*

A form of shareware in which the software's author asks you to send your registration fee to a designated charity instead of to him or her.

carrier   Technical Term   *Noun*

(1) A provider of phone service. This term might get a big frisky in the coming years, seeing as technology and legislation have progressed to the point where your Internet provider, your cable company, and your local Baby Bell can give you phone service.

(2) The basic "noise" which modems generate when talking to each other. Once two modems establish this carrier tone among themselves, they can impress another signal upon it to transmit and receive data.

Think of the carrier as a clothesline strung between your modem and the modem of the machine you're connecting to and the data are sheets of notepaper that you clip to the clothesline. When this carrier signal is lost (usually because there's been a big disruption on your phone line), the connection between the two modems is lost along with it.

CCITT   Organization   *Noun*

Oh, Lord … OK: Comité Consultatif International Télégraphique et Téléphonique. Well, it's not important. All you need to remember is that this is the international committee which decides and certifies international standards for communications. Actually, it's a lot of fun to pronounce in an Inspector Clouseau-ish voice. Try it now, won't you?

CERT   Organization   *Noun*

Computer Emergency Response Team. A government-funded organization that investigates and disseminates information about Internet security. Sort of like the BATF for the Internet, only they're not quite so intense.

CFV   Online Jargon   *Noun*

Call For Votes. A CFC (Call for Comments) is announced whenever someone has proposed that a new Usenet newsgroup be established. The Internet community can then vote on whether or not they think Usenet really needs a discussion group for Icelandic polka music, by sending e-mail to a specified address.

CGI   Technical Term   *Noun*

Common Gateway Interface. Either a program or a link to a program on a webserver that a webpage (but not the webpage's user) can access. CGIs allow web-pages to be "live" in some way or another, or to respond to the actions of the user. A webpage which displays a live picture of the room the webserver is in, for instance, might use a CGI to automatically trigger an electronic camera and display the image whenever the page is accessed. Ditto for most "search" web-pages, which return a list of links to sites of interest: the CGI builds a brand-new webpage from scratch with the requested links.

chat   Technical Term   *Noun*

"Live" talk, generally just between two people. What you type appears on the other person's screen and vice versa. *See Also*: **conference**

checksum   Technical Term   *Noun*

Refers to a very general scheme for detecting errors in a stream of data. Simply put, the sender and the receiver does some math on the actual numbers being transmitted, and pauses to make sure that they both wound up with the same answer. If these two checksums don't match, that means the batch of numbers transmitted was not identical to the batch received.

chipset   Technical Term   *Noun*

The firmware of a modem. These are special chips that contain all of the low-level software a modem needs to operate (protocols for data transmission, compression, error-detection, etc.) and the modem manufacturer generally buys these ready-made from an outside company. Modems are often advertised as having such-and-such's chipset, indicating that it has more or less the same capabilities as any other modem with the same chipset. Common chipsets offer another advantage in that software that controls one modem with a certain chipset will usually control any modem with that chipset. For instance, if your America Online software does not have a pre-defined configuration for your DiscoModem28.8, the configuration for the LambadaComStar v.34 will work just as well if the two modems have the same chipset. *See Also:* **Rockwell, AT&T**

chooser   Technical Term   *Noun*

In the Macintosh operating system, the Chooser is an item under the Apple menu that allows you to choose among the various devices available to you on the network, typically file servers and printers, though other devices can be chosen as well.

CI$ Online Jargon   *Noun*

Slightly derogatory term for CompuServe. This dates way back to when access charges were relatively enormous, and is no longer really applicable.

ciphertext   Technical Term   *Noun*

Encrypted text. *See Also:* **plaintext**

CIS   Online Entity   *Noun*

See Instead: **CompuServe**

ClariNet   Online Entity   *Noun*

Sort of a commercial fiefdom of Usenet; newsgroups in the clari. hierarchy contain commercial information, like the Reuters newswire, syndicated columns and comic strips, etc.

client   Technical Term   *Noun*

A database term that refers to a machine that chiefly, just receives information from a server. This has been perverted a bit for online use, to refer to a machine that logs onto a larger machine. For instance, when you log onto America Online, your computer is acting as a client, and the custom software you're using to access the service is known as client software. Not technically an accurate application of the term, but it's been published in *InfoWorld* now so I guess we're stuck with it.

Clipper Chip   Technical Term   *Noun*

A security chip that the government wanted installed in every single piece of communications hardware—phones, fax machines, modems, the whole ball of wax. Supposedly it encrypted your communications so that the general public couldn't easily listen in, but in reality each Clipper Chip would have had a backdoor the government could use to monitor your communications. OK, yes, only with a warrant, but still it was a pretty bogus concept. Largely a dead technology, thanks largely to public outcry.

cloak   Online Jargon   *Verb*

To hack a message so that its valid source information is stripped and the receiver therefore cannot determine who sent it. *See Also:* **morphing, remailer**

clone   Technical Term   *Noun*

A computer which is designed to run the same software as another company's computer. This term used to refer exclusively to machines that could run IBM PC software but weren't manufactured by IBM, but

<color> box **41**

before long "real" IBM PC's were resoundingly out-
numbered by IBM clones, and that's when the Industry
started referring to "Windows software" instead of
"IBM PC software." Today, the term more often than
not refers to machines which can run the MacOS but
aren't manufactured by Apple, as Apple has only
recently begun licensing its hardware technologies to
other computer manufacturers.

coax   Technical Term   *Noun*

A thick, sturdy type of cable used for broad-band-
width communications. Beloved in the geek community. Just as tool geeks praise duct tape for being able to
keep any two objects fastened together, tech geeks
praise coax for physically being able to keep any two
pieces of data hardware in reliable communications.
The mind staggers at the metaphysical possibilities
suggested by the image of hooking up two computers
with coax and then duct-taping them together.

CODEC   Technical Term   *Noun*

Compressor-Decompressor. General term for the
algorithm that compresses a stream of data at one
end of a transmission and decompresses it at the
other end. Usually refers to video and audio signals.

<color> box   Online Jargon   *Noun*

In phreaking circles, a pocketable home-made electronic gizmo designed to exploit specific weaknesses in a public service, usually the phone system. Each color refers to a specific set of features; for instance, a red box fools pay phones into thinking that you've just dumped in a boatload of quarters, a silver box is for fooling the photosensor in a modern traffic light into thinking that you're an ambulance and need a green light right away, etc.

.com   Online Entity   *Noun*

See Instead: **domain**

comm   Technical Term   *Noun/Adjective*

Communications. Usually used in combinations, such as "comm software."

comp   Online Entity   *Noun*

See Instead: **newsgroup**

Compactor Pro   Product   *Noun*

The other archive format for Macintosh, though its popularity is rather negligible; Stuffit is the de facto standard.

compatible   Online Jargon   *Noun*

Salesman-speak for "something I bet I can sell you because you've told me you already own…" as in "This EISA-based modem card is compatible with your Power Macintosh."

component software
Technical Term   *Noun*

An emerging concept in software in which you can exploit a needed feature of a program without actually having to be within that program's environment. The classic example would be a word processing document (an annual report, say) which contains a table of financial data from a spreadsheet. Currently, you'd do your calculations in a spreadsheet program, select the resulting numbers, and cut and paste them into your report, having to go back into the spreadsheet if the numbers change later. With component software, the spreadsheet program can "lend" the word processor enough of its features that you can just correct the table right in the report itself. Component Software, much like life, will either totally revolutionize everything or turn out to be a complete waste of collective time and effort. *See Also:* **OLE, OpenDoc**

CompuServe   Online Entity   *Noun*

The second largest commercial online service behind AOL, and also the oldest service which remains a real player in the marketplace. Why subscribe to CompuServe: CIS's greatest advantage is its remarkable signal-to-noise ratio, far and away the highest of any online service. It could be stated that CIS is the only major online service on which actual, literate conversation takes place, as opposed to strangers exchanging e-mail. All forums are very well moderated and standards of conduct are strictly enforced, which has led to a very civilized and clubby atmosphere. CompuServe also offers the widest breadth of services. In addition to the expected enormous number of public forums, CIS offers connections to dozens of research databases and services; it is possible to write a message and then have a CompuServe entity translate it into Japanese and then snail-mail it to its destination. Finally (and least relevant to most readers) users have the option of accessing the service with either CompuServe's simplified graphical client software, special "Navigator" programs which let you read and reply to messages and select files to download while not actually connected to the service (thus saving you boatloads of cash), or even plain text terminal programs (which means that in an emergency, you could even get your mail using your personal organizer if you really needed to). Why you shouldn't subscribe to CompuServe: the learning curve. Unlike the nearly preschoolish ease of AOL, CIS takes a little longer to master, even when using the service's free graphical interface client. Phun Phact: CompuServe is owned lock, stock, and barrel by H&R Block.

conference   Technical Term   *Noun*

Like Chat, except it refers typically to live online talk among a large group of people instead of between just two. Participants enter a special "conference room" in which comments appear on everyone's screens simultaneously. *See Also:* **chat**

content   Technical Term   *Noun*

The industrial bourgeoisie's latest blatant attempt to marginalize the invaluable contributions of writers, artists, animators, and musicians, by coming up with this antiseptic word to describe the text, artwork, animation, and music that is created and made available on the Net.

Control-L   Online Jargon   *Verb/Noun*

To insert a special "Spoiler" character into a message so that for instance, no one who hasn't seen *The Crying Game* will accidentally read onward and find out that the dame is actually a guy. In many UNIX newsreaders, a control-L is actually the keystroke for inserting a Spoiler. Oh, and my apologies if you were planning on seeing that movie later.

cookie   Technical Term   *Noun*

A small file that a webpage creates on your hard drive. These files contain innocuous stuff; a web-based adventure game, for instance, might create a cookie that records where you were and what you were carrying when you last quit the game. It should be pointed out, though, that the concept of a webpage-creating files on a hard drive without the user's permission gives some people a roaring case of the heebie-jeebies.

CPS   Technical Term   *Noun*

Characters Per Second. Unlike BPS, the CPS speed reflects factors like the length of each character (7 or 8 bits), data compression, and the like. As a rule of thumb, if you multiply the CPS rate by ten you're left with the "effective" BPS rate. For instance, let's say you connect to CompuServe with your v.34 modem at 28,800 bits per second, and the modem's data compression manages to squeeze the data you're downloading by fifty percent. Your BPS rate (which steadfastly counts just the bits of information being transmitted) remained at 28,800, but the data will be received at a speed of 4,320 CPS, which is like having a 43,200 BPS modem. *See Also:* **BPS**

.CPT   Technical Term   *Noun*

File extension for Compactor Pro file archive.

cracker   Online Jargon   *Noun*

Vile miscreant who tries to break into systems without authorization. *See Also:* **hacker, phreak**

crash and burn   Online Jargon   *Noun*

A system crash which is almost a glory to behold, with

pulsating colors on the screen and a flurry of sound coming out of the speakers, for instance. In other words, what happens to a computer in the movies when Jerry Lewis or Don Knotts pushes any one button at random.

CRC Technical Term *Noun*

Cyclical Redundancy Checking. A form of checksum that forms the backbone of most error-checking protocols. CRC involves adding together all of the numbers sent in one burst, dividing the number by 69,665 and comparing the mathematical remainder to the one the transmitter sent along with the data. Sixty-nine thousand six hundred and sixty-four is a magic number because due to the vagaries of binary math and data communications, using it traps all but 0.002% of all possible errors, which is close enough for government work, as they say. By three orders of magnitude.

crippleware Technical Term *Noun*

Almost a synonym of demoware, except it's usually used to refer to shareware that has most of its tastier features disabled until it's "unlocked" with a special code you can only get by sending in the shareware fee. See Also: public domain software, shareware, demoware, pimpware

crosspost Online Jargon *Noun/Verb*

To post a single message to more than one newsgroup. Exciting new pictures of Shatner's new hair-piece might be crossposted to alt.fan.shatner, rec.arts.star-trek, and soc.bald-guys. When you cross-post a message, you send one copy of that message along with pointers for each newsgroup you're send-ing it to. This saves space. Individually sending an identi-cal message to several newsgroups wastes space, and is often considered spam. Inappropriate crossposting is also often considered spam. See Also: **spam**

crufty   Online Jargon   *Adjective*

Too big, too complicated, utterly inelegant, looks like it'll crumble to bits if you so much as look at it funny.

crunchy   Online Jargon   *Adjective*

Used to describe hippies or (more often) a hippie wannabe. 'Cause hippies eat a lot of granola, and gra-nola's crunchy, y'dig?

Example | No, I don't hang out on alt.music.grate-ful-dead. Too crunchy for my taste.

CSLIP   Technical Term   *Noun*

A faster version of SLIP which incorporates compres-sion of both data and header info. Not all ISPs sup-port CSLIP.

CUL8R   Online Jargon   *Interjection*

See You Later.

cu-cme   Product   *Noun*

Freeware program which lets you conduct live video-conferencing, either on a one-to-one basis or as part of a group. All that's required is a video camera connected to your computer (like Connectix' QuickCam), an Internet connection, and the cu-cme software (or its commercial equivalent, produced by White Pine Software). In the case of a "direct" one-to-one call, you connect directly with your target, while in a group configuration you connect to a "reflector site" tasked to hosting the group.

cyber-   Online Jargon   *Noun*

Prefix meaning "computer." In the name of a commercial product or service, usually denotes a cynical and ill-informed attempt by Big Business to make some quick bucks.

Cyberdog   Product   *Noun*

As soon as the word "Internet" became indelibly linked to the phrase "gravy train," every major player in the computer industry scrambled to announce that they were developing a Killer Internet Technology.

Apple seems to be one of the few which actually delivered. Cyberdog is a fundamental new part of the Macintosh Operating System which allows Internet functions to be pasted into a document in almost exactly the same way that graphics and video can. Need to include a photo in that company report you're writing? Don' tell the reader to launch a graphics program and open a specific graphic file...just paste the photo right into the document. Similarly, instead of writing "Every day the NOAA posts a weather advisory for small craft. To get today's report, launch Netscape and access the following URL:", write "Here is the today's NOAA small craft advisory:" and paste in a Cyberdog browser pointing to that same URL.

Trust me, it's way cool. You can get more info on Cyberdog at http://cyberdog.apple.com/.

cyberpunk   Online Jargon   *Noun*

(1) A term that debuted in William Gibson's SF classic *Neuromancer,* which in the parlance refers to an entire category of techno-science fiction and its devotées.

(2) The sort of person who has read all about the Internet in *Newsweek* and based on the fact that s/he owns a computer and a pager and knows where s/he can buy a copy of *2600* starts demanding that people start calling him 8888SynestorPPC. Someone who owns the entire multi-volume set of *Inside Macintosh* technical documentation but doesn't know that the power switch is on the keyboard and not the computer.

cyberspace   Online Jargon   *Noun*

What cyberpunks and *Newsweek* say when they mean
to say "the Net."

cyberzine   Online Jargon   *Noun*

A magazine that is available exclusively online, typically
on the Web.

Cypherpunk   Online Jargon   *Noun*

Part of the growing segment of the Internet community which is doggedly concerned about privacy issues.
Cypherpunks believe, among other things, that the
average user ought to have access to the most powerful encryption software available and that if the average Internet user wants their communications to be
absolutely private, well, that should be their decision.
This concept rankles certain factions within The
Gummint, who for various reasons sleep a little more
soundly knowing that if one of its 300,000,000 citizens
were planning to detonate a home-made nuclear
weapon and bragged about his plans to a friend and
used either the Internet or a cellular phone to do so
and encrypted their communications and the aforementioned Gummint Faction happened to have had a
tap on his communications, then they would be able
to decrypt the message without having to ask the
Citizen for his encryption key.
    Toward that end, The Gummint wishes its citizens
to only have access to encryption schemes which are

just slightly more complicated than Pig Latin. And this sort of thing really gets up the Cypherpunks' noses, so to speak.

Das Blinkenlights   Online Jargon   *Noun*

Ancient term referring to the myriad blinking lights on old mainframes. Still popular today to refer to any sort of blinking indicator lights, particularly ones just there to make the machine look cool. Check out the Thinking Machines supercomputer in *Jurassic Park* for a classic set of Blinkenlights.

DCE   Technical Term   *Noun*

Data Circuit-Terminating Equipment. A piece of hardware that connects one computer (more appropriately, one DTE) to another. Usually a DCE refers to a modem.

debbie   · Online Jargon   *Noun*

Newbies who are pig-ignorant, unmannered philistines primarily because of their inexperience. If someone's a certified flamer, well, hog-pile on him and administer the pummeling he so richly deserves. A debbie, on the other hand, can be rehabilitated with patience and mild, corrective electric shocks.

de facto   Technical Term   *Adjective*

A standard which came to pass because, well, every-one was doing it, as opposed to the CCITT standards that were bashed out after lots of intelligent people on a committee spent a whole year sending each other violently argumentative e-mail. What you have to watch out for about de facto standards is that sometimes folks will try to convince you they're more important than they really are. It doesn't matter if CorelDraw is "the de facto standard for professional graphics on Windows" according to some guy you met; if you prefer Adobe Illustrator, then go with it.

defenestrate   Online Jargon   *Verb*

To throw out of a window. Popular in newsgroups, also serves as ample evidence that there's a word for everything.

DejaNews   Online Entity   *Noun*

An Internet search engine for searching mountains of Usenet postings for ones containing specified key-words. Really useful. http://www.dejanews.com/.

demoware   Technical Term   *Noun*

A special "limited" version of a software package

which can be downloaded and used like freeware. Key features of the product are disabled (the ability to save or print your work, typically) so that the demo-ware gives you the opportunity to get a real feel for the product and its capabilities without relieving you of the need to actually buy the complete, commercial version. Sometimes referred to as "crippleware." *See Also:* **public domain software, shareware, pimpware, crippleware**

DES   Technical Term   *Noun*

Data Encryption Standard. An old (and therefore widespread and also antiquated) scheme for encrypting data. It quickly fell out of favor when the rumor spread that The Gummint intentionally crippled DES so that while encrypted data remained safe by any reasonable or conceivably unreasonable attempt to crack the code without the right password, the encryption was still simple enough for the National Security Agency to crash through. (Remember, the ocean is wet, the sun is hot, and the NSA has enough computing hardware to calculate where you were on your seventh birthday just by analyzing a wad of gum found under a chair in a bus station in Dayton. And you've never even been to Dayton.) Pretty much obsoleted by RSA, a scheme which offers more features and better protection.

desktop   Technical Term   *Noun*

A computer which sits on your desk and is leashed to a wall outlet.

/dev/null   Online Jargon   *Noun*

In the UNIX file system, the directory /dev/null is a black hole into which things disappear. Used similarly as a colloquialism.

Example ┃ ```
         ┃ Look, I really wish you'd take your
         ┃ rambling 928-line "BAYWATCH is way
         ┃ better than LOVE BOAT" posting and
         ┃ route it straight to /dev/null, OK?
```

## dialer   Technical Term   *Noun*

A program that dials your ISP and actually establishes a PPP or SLIP connection. Because TCP software only has the means with which to exploit a connection and not the means to create it, this outside program is necessary.

## dialup, dialup access
Technical Term   *Noun*

A connection to the Internet that requires a phone be dialed at your end, as opposed to a hardwire connection. Sometimes (and incorrectly) used to refer to a shell account.

## digest   Technical Term   *Noun*

(1) A special kind of electronic mailing list consisting of
```

particularly good postings and discussions from a newsgroup. This allows you to follow the meat of a newsgroup without having to slog through hundreds of postings a day.

(2) A method of receiving a mailing list where a lot of messages are all sent in one batch. This way, if you're on a really active list, you will get one huge message a day, instead of 117 individual e-mails.

digital   Online Jargon   *Adjective*

Technically, refers to a signal which consists of a series of "ons" and "offs"— any signal which passes through a computer. In the vernacular it refers to something existing in the online world ("The company will have a digital presence by the end of the year."), or something which is intrinsically easy to break down and understand. *See Also:* **analog**

discussion list   Technical Term   *Noun*

A "many to many" mailing list in which a reply sent to this bit of e-mail is sent to every subscriber of that mailing list. It's sort of a hybrid between a public newsgroup and private mail; it's like a newsgroup which is "invitation only."

DNRC   Online Jargon   *Noun*

Dogbert's New Ruling Class. I'd explain further, but if you're worthy of inclusion then you probably don't need me to. In fact, you probably don't need this book. Hmm?

DNS   Technical Term   *Noun*

Domain Name System. The Internet's standard method for connecting names with addresses. Instead of having to maintain a log of IP numbers (each one being a string of numbers separated by periods…hard to remember) a person or company establishing a machine on the Net can register a name (tango.lambada.com). Whenever anyone on the Internet tries to connect to this machine, his machine contacts a DNS server which tells it that tango.lambada.com is the machine at 192.03.182.2 and, bang, they're off and running. Almost all of this name-registration business is handled by InterNIC, at http://internic.net/.

dogcow   Online Jargon   *Noun*

The unofficial mascot of the Macintosh; the familiar half-dog, half-cow you see in the "Print Options" dialog.

domain   Online Entity   *Noun*

(1) In an internet address, the parts to the right of the @ symbol. In the address andyi@world.std.com, the items separated by periods describe (in decreasing order of specificity) where, physically, on the Internet this entity can be located. ".com" is, technically, the only

true "domain" in this address, and they describe what sort of organization this address belongs to:

> .com—A commercial entity. Typically a business or Internet service provider.
>
> .edu—Educational, typically a college or university.
>
> .gov—The Gummint.
>
> .mil—The military.
>
> .net—Organizations involved in the Internet as a whole
>
> .org—Everything else.

The other items in this list are Subdomains and will vary. In this case, std refers to Software Tool & Die, the company which owns this Internet site, and World refers to The World, the division of Software Tool and Die which provides Internet service to schmoes like me. There are also "country" domains, found at the end of addresses depending on which country your host machine is located in. ".jp" tells you that this entity is located in Japan, ".uk" means it's in Great Britain, etc.

(2) That of God which scientists in Fifties science fiction films declared they should not tamper in, just before the end credits.

dongle   Online Jargon   *Noun*

Generic term for any little box the size of a box of matches or a pack of cigarettes which hangs off one of your computer's ports via a short cable. Ethernet and LocalTalk connectors are usually referred to as dongles, as are certain uncouth little hardware gizmos that act as physical "keys," which permit a specific piece of copy-protected software to run on a specific machine. Beastly things.

DOS   Product   *Noun*

Disk Operating System. (1) The text-based operating system that is the native OS of Intel-based PCs. Windows is "purty," but, when you get right down to it, it's just a fancy front-end to DOS.

(2) A concept by which we measure our pain.

dot path   Online Jargon   *Noun*

Modern, Internet-style address, like world.std.com, in which domains are separated by periods. *See Also:* **bang path**

down   Online Jargon   *Adjective*

Not functional right now but will be functional again sometime in the future. "I'm sorry, my conversational wetware is down right now…could I call you back in an hour or two?"

download   Technical Term   *Verb/Noun*

To receive a file from an online host. Often used as a noun, as in, "This game is the hottest download of the week." Also often corrupted to refer to any transfer of a file, whether you're sending or receiving. Folks who care about such things—all of you, I reckon—will nonetheless only use this term to refer to receiving data. *See Also:* **upload**

driver   Technical Term   *Noun*

A piece of system-level software which allows the operating system to work with a specific piece of hardware.

DTE   Technical Term   Noun

Data Terminal Equipment. An acronym you usually only see in your modem's manual and in certain right-eously geeky comm newsgroups. Refers to the hard-ware which generates data sent over a data communi-cations device. The computer plugged into your modem, for instance, is a DTE.

DTMF   Technical Term   *Noun*

Dual Tone Multi Frequency. The method used to gen-erate touch-tone tones.

duty-cycle   Technical Term   *Noun*

Technically, the minimum unit of time in which a com-puter can do something. We're talking something basic, like take a number from memory and move it into the microprocessor. Colloquially, used to refer to capacity for work; as in "Well, this machine just has more duty-cycles available." Most popularly used to refer to a human's wetware capacity. "I realized that I was wasting duty-cycles every time I brush my teeth, so I have all of my e-mail piped to a screen in my bathroom."

E   Online Jargon   *Adjective*

Good old-fashioned mathematical notation indicating the number ten raised to a certain power. "ThanksE6!" is a "cute" way of saying "Thanks a million!"

EBCDIC   Technical Term   *Noun*

(A little self-indulgent, I know, but please take just a half a second here to acknowledge how having to spend an entire week researching and writing nothing but obscure acronyms does have the net effect of battering the soul somewhat. Just a little understanding of the effort involved, that's all I ask.) Extended Binary Coded Decimal Interchange Code. The standard for encoding characters into numbers that is not ASCII. No one uses this standard any more and it only pops up in conversation when the poster is feeling nostalgic or is using it to be derisive.

Echo   Technical Term   *Noun*

(1) As a communication parameter, when "Echo" or

"Local Echo" is on, the computer will display everything you type in the terminal window. Normally, whichever host you're connected to sends the characters you type back to you as you type them, so if you have this feature turned on when you don't need it, what you type wwiillll lloooookk lliikkee tthhiiss.

(2) On FidoNet, the rough equivalent of Usenet newsgroups.

(3) A BBS based in New York City with lots of journalists and a higher ratio of women and older folk than you often see on the Net. Stands for East Coast Hang-Out. http://www.echonyc.com.

.edu   Online Entity   *Noun*

See *Instead:* **domain**

ELF   Technical Term   *Noun*

See *Instead:* **EMF**

elite   Online Jargon   *Adjective*

Refers to the seamier side of the hacking experience. Therefore, an "elite" BBS would be a BBS which features pirated software, utilities for cracking passwords, lists of stolen credit card numbers, phreak files, etc.

elm   Product   *Noun*

More or less the standard UNIX mailreader for folks who use shell access to the Internet.

Emacs   Technical Term   *Noun*

God looked down upon the Earth, and saw frenzy and discord; and He reflected that perhaps the people needed tangible and incontriverable evidence of His presence and His love of the Earth and its denizens; and so He smoked the ground and up from the Earth sprung Richard Stallman, who wrote the Emacs text editor. Or so thousands of Emacs fans would tell it. Emacs is legendary for being a text editor that can be set up to do absolutely anything. Write code, read e-mail, follow newsgroups…the fact that it has an entire programming language built into it means that it does whatever programmers want it to do, and programmers want it to do just about everything.

e-mail   Technical Term   *Noun/Verb*

Technically speaking, e-mail is any message transmitted electronically. However, it's most popularly used to refer to a message sent to a private mailbox as opposed to one posted in a public message forum.

EMF   Technical Term   *Noun*

Electromagnetic Field; any electrical current generates

an accompanying electromagnetic field. One of a half-dozen hot potato health worries of folks who pound keyboards for a living. Almost every electronic device emits an EMF, and there have been studies linking prolonged exposure to EMF to certain cancers. The jury's definitely still out on this subject, but nonetheless folks who spend ten hours a day with their heads three feet away from the back of the monster monitor of the guy in the cubicle behind them want to know more about this. Of particular concern are ELF (Extremely Low Frequency) emissions, found near high-power lines.

emoticons   Online Style   *Interjection*

When speaking with someone face-to-face, the person's facial expressions help you understand the meaning of what he or she is saying. Emoticons are an attempt to bring that extra nuance to online communications, by composing a face out of ASCII characters. The most utilitarian emoticons are (tilt your head to the left):

:-)	Happy/smiling, or "I'm just kidding." This is the most useful emoticon of them all, as it prevents people from misinterpreting your message as a genuine insult or a serious answer to something.
;-)	Winking
:-(	Sad
>:-<	Angry
:-P	Sticking my tongue out at you.

:-o   Shocked. Or perhaps just whistling.

:-*   Delivering a kiss.

:^(My nose is out of joint.

(It is also popular to truncate the Happy and Sad emoticons to only two characters each, as in :) or :(. This allows
the emotion to be communicated with an immediate 33%
increase in transmission speed, which will appeal to almost
any true online aficionado.) There are also hundreds of far,
far more baroque variations, usually written for the amusement of the sender and not the aid of the reader, as in:

#-)   I'm drunk.

B-)   I've got my shades on…I'm a cool dude.

::-)   I wear eyeglasses. (Four eyes. Get it?)

<:)   I'm acting like clown.

+-<:-)   I am the Pope.

NB: Try to keep your stick on the ice when it comes
to emoticons. A :) or a :(is a simple and effective way.
Many regard emoticons as the online equivalent of
dotting your i's with little happy faces, and if you liber-
ally pepper your messages with them you'll be pegged
as a hapless newbie. Though personally I'm rather fond
of the old-world charm of @>—-`——,——, which is
the ASCII equivalent of presenting someone with a
long-stemmed rose. See Also: grin

Example | Yes, it _is_ "Spring Back, Fall
Forward." So don't forget to set
your clock an hour _ahead_ this
weekend, and good luck on that big
job interview. :)

enclosure   Technical Term   *Noun*

See *Instead:* **attachment**

encryption   Technical Term   *Noun*

The process of encoding a message so that it cannot be read if intercepted by a third party. As civil libertarians, plain honest folk, and paranoids start hopping on the Internet, encryption has become a hot area of development.

engine   Technical Term   *Noun*

A piece of code that doesn't do anything on its own but acts as a resource for other software. For instance, on Macintosh computers, the Stuffit Engine contains every conceivable piece of code needed for compressing and decompressing files, and so if it's present, any comm program (like Netscape) can automatically decompress any file you download with it. A more universal Internet concept is the "search engine," a set of code on a host computer which can search for information on the Web, Usenet, or other Internet entities. You, the user don't interact with the engine directly, but use software (a web search page) which in turn interacts with the engine.

EOF   Technical Term   *Noun*

End Of File. The marker in a file that tells your software "there ain't nothing more to read." On a badly munged file, you might get an "Unexpected EOF Error," which means that the software encountered the EOF marker before it was finished reading data.

.eps   Technical Term   *Noun*

File extension for encapsulated Postscript graphics.

Ethernet   Technical Term   *Noun*

The most popular standard for wiring a bunch of computers together into a network.

Eudora   Product   *Noun*

Qualcomm product that has become the standard mailreader software for both Mac and Windows. Though there are plenty of freeware, shareware, and commercial alternatives, the fact that Eudora is available in both commercial and freeware versions and is supported by just about everyone has given it an impressive foothold.

EvangeList   Online Jargon   *Noun*

Guy Kawasaki's frighteningly large and influential list-server, whose purpose is to provide Macintosh lovers with all of the ammunition they need to convince a fickly and cloth-eared populace to embrace Macintosh computers.

.exe   Technical Term   *Noun*

File extension for an executible DOS or Windows program.

Exon   Online Jargon   *Noun*

A democratic senator with an eye toward cheap publicity decided to draft a rider to the Telecommunications Act that would have placed unconstitutional restrictions on the sort of speech you can conduct on the Internet. This was done under the cozy umbrella of "Protecting Our Children From Indecency." This also tended to tick people off, people who care about freedom and stuff like that, and so Dilbert cartoonist Scott Adams announced that from now on, whenever he felt motivated to use vulgar language on the Internet, instead of exposing "the kids" to such words he'd substitute the name of a Congressperson. Hence, you might come across a Usenet posting in which one individual urges the other to "Go Exon Yourself."

facetime   Online Jargon   *Noun*

Time spent physically standing in the room with someone and talking with them. Most netters intend to try
this out some time.

fan key   Online Jargon   *Noun*

On Macintoshes, the button with the symbol on it
that looks like a four-way cloverleaf interchange.
Roughly equivalent to the ALT key on Wintel keyboards. Also called the command key.

FAQ   Online Jargon   *Noun*

Short for Frequently Asked Question. In any online
forum that has been active for a great deal of time
(particularly a Usenet newsgroup), there are questions
that get asked fairly regularly (such as "So, does
Shatner wear a toupee or what?" on a "Star Trek"
forum). Oftentimes, these questions are collected into
a "FAQ File," or "FAQ" for short, and updated as
needed. It is considered good etiquette to consult the
forum's FAQ file before posting a question which you
suspect has been asked a million times before.

faxmodem   Technical Term   *Noun*

A modem that is also capable of sending and receiving

faxes. This used to be a bit of a tony item, but the feature became so popular and the chips so cheap to produce that it's more economical for a manufacturer to include fax features in all of its modems than to maintain two separate product lines.

FidoNet   Technical Term   *Noun*

A part of the Net made up of BBS's running the Fido BBS software.

file extension   Technical Term   *Noun*

A suffix added to a file name that describes the file's contents. The extension, usually three characters long, is separated from the file name by a period. Examples are *.gif,* the extension for the GIF picture format, and *.uu,* the extension for a uuencoded file.

finger   Technical Term   *Noun/Verb*

Internet resource that lets you determine whether or not a specific user is online right now or when he or she was last signed on. If the person has defined a finger file, you might receive other pertinent info (office hours, phone numbers, a witty saying about food, etc.). Can also be used to pull a list of everyone currently logged into a specific host machine.

firewall   Technical Term   *Noun*

General term referring to the warren's nest of security software and procedures that protects a system from the invasion of unauthorized users. Almost every system's firewalls are different, which in theory limits the effectiveness of any one vile miscreant. A firewall often has other consequences as well, such as preventing users from being fingered or rendering certain network software nonfunctional.

firmware   Technical Term   *Noun*

Software that arrives burned onto chips as opposed to on disk or CD or installed on a hard drive. This is low-level, fundamental software, routines which the hardware needs the instant you switch it on. Babies, for instance, arrive from the factory with just basic software in firmware that it needs on start-up: routines for breathing, eating, corresponding bodily functions, crying, and learning. It's this basic core library of routines that allows more complicated and practical software to load in. With modems, you usually talk of firmware in terms of the protocols the unit has. With the better models, the firmware is upgradable, so your pokey v.32bis modem can be made to be "Thoroughly Modern" at minimal expense. Colloqually, firmware is also used to refer to a quality that is part of something's fundamental nature and can't be overriden:

Example | No, Steve can't wake up any earlier than 11 A.M.; it's part of the firmware.

FirstClass   Product   *Noun*

A commercial Bulletin Board Service (BBS) software package that allows the creation of graphical user interfaces. With the explosion of the Internet, the product's been repositioned as a solution for bringing Internet-like services to standard office networks.

flag   Technical Term   *Noun*

A variable with exactly two possible settings, usually On or Off, Yes or No. CompuServe forum sysops can manipulate a "Free Flag," for each of the forum's users for instance; if yours is "on," then you aren't charged for the time you spend in the forum.

flame bait   Online Jargon   *Noun*

A posting posted to entice flamers, designed to get people so steamed that they reply to it. See Also: troll

flamer   Online Jargon   *Noun*

A person who engages in flaming. A vile miscreant. *See Also:* **flaming**

flaming   Online Jargon   *Noun*

Responding to a public message with the sort of bile

and venom which is only appropriate when someone makes scandalous and unforgivable remarks regarding your mother. Typically, a flamer does this for the same reason that some prankers pull fire alarms: It's a simple action that results in an enormous reaction the flamer, somehow, finds amusing. The only proven method for getting a flamer to shut up and go away is to ignore him or her.

NB: Some newbies believe that flaming is just part of the fun of online communications. Be advised that there are few breaches of online etiquette worse than this one, and repeated flaming will cause your sysop to close down your account. *See Also:* **trolling**

flashROM   Technical Term   *Noun*

A special kind of read-only memory which can actually be rewritten under the right circumstances. A nifty feature in modems, in that it lets you fix bugs in the firmware or add new features without having to send the modem back to the factory for a new set of ROMs.

Flower Key   Online Jargon   *Noun*

See *Instead:* **fan key**

FOAF   Online Jargon   *Noun*

Friend Of A Friend. As in, "Well, you might think that no one's ever found a dead mouse inside a soda bottle, but a FOAF actually…'' Intentionally or unintentionally sends the message that this story might actually be true.

followup   Online Jargon   *Noun*

On Usenet, a public posting generated in response to another posting.

fora   Online Jargon   *Noun*

Plural of forum.

foreground   Online Jargon   *Noun*

Technically, in a multitasking operating system, the application you're currently working with, as opposed to those which are in the background. Colloquially, your full and complete attention, which can be focused on only one thing at a time. If your roomate is complaining to you about the phone bill while you're browsing a newsgroup online, the Internet is your foreground process. *See Also:* **background**

forklift upgrade   Online Jargon   *Noun*

The sort of last-ditch upgrade which involves just throwing away the computer you have and buying a new one. Usually the most economical course of action, in fact.

forum   Online Jargon   *Noun*

A conglomeration of online people communicating with each other. Can refer to a section of a commercial service dedicated to a specific topic (such as the SHOWBIZ forum on CompuServe), a newsgroup on Usenet, or just as readily to a live conference.

forward   Technical Term   *Noun/Verb*

Means just what it means in real life: to send a copy of an electronic message you've received to a third party. Normally this is a basic function of your mail-reader software.

frames   Technical Term   *Noun*

A much hated Netscape-specific addition to HTML, which allows the browser window to be split into multiple, independent sections. Hated because pages that use frames can't be bookmarked properly, and, generally speaking, it forces the user to waste valuable screen real estate with a panel of buttons or a dopey banner which they no longer need to look at.

FreePPP   Product   *Noun*

A freeware (and therefore insanely popular) set of system extensions for bringing PPP services to the Macintosh.

freeware   Technical Term   *Noun*

Software the author has decided to make available to the online community free of charge. You don't have to pay to obtain it (beyond the nominal charge of downloading a file), you're free to hand out copies to friends, and you're not expected to send in a registration fee.

NB: There's an important difference between freeware and public domain software. Software that has been released into the public domain belongs to no one; the copyright belongs to the public at large and as such anyone (or any company) can do absolutely whatever they want with the software. If a program is freeware, the original author retains the copyright and, as such, can limit its use and distribution, e.g., sue the bejeezus out of a company which decides to slap it on a disk and charge a hundred bucks for it. *See Also:* **shareware, demoware, pimpware**

freeze   Online Jargon   *Noun*

A maddeningly subdued system crash in which apparently the keyboard and mouse stop working and all activity on the screen ceases; in a macabre fashion, your computer is a living snapshot of your last unclaimed opportunity to save that important report that's due in an hour.

Also refers to the moment you stop adding features to a project; "OK, let's freeze the design, finish coding, and ship this product!"

fried   Online Jargon   *Adjective*

Of hardware, actually physically burned-out, with cool smoke and smells and everything. Of people, overworked to the point of taking away their car keys and their Swiss Army knife and getting them a cab home.

ftp   Technical Term   *Noun/Verb*

File Transfer Protocol, the standard protocol for sending a file from one computer to another. ftp is the "lingua franca" of the Internet, while bulletin boards and online services may offer as many as a dozen different protocols to choose from, almost all file transfers on the Internet itself are done with ftp.

NB: ftp is both the name of the protocol and the Unix program which actually executes the transfer. It can also be used as a verb.

Example

```
I ftp'ed the updates to my web-
server this afternoon, so you can
take a look at them any time now.
```

FUD   Online Jargon   *Noun*

Fear, Uncertainty, and Doubt; one of the many factors which causes wussy corporate types to make awful decisions. The FUD Factor is popularly used to explain why IBM sold so many mainframes. That middle manager couldn't understand the features of all the different systems, and ultimately decided that nobody ever got fired for buying an IBM. Today, it's more applicable to the success of Microsoft.

fudge factor   Online Jargon   *Noun*

Margin for error one way or another.

FWIW   Online Jargon   *Interjection*

For What It's Worth. Popular abbreviation in electronic messages.

FYA   Online Jargon   *Noun*

For Your Amusement.

g   Online Style   *Interjection*

See *Instead:* **grin**

ga   Online Style   *Interjection*

During a one-on-one chat, typed at the end of a line to signal the other person that you've finished your thought and they can now type a response without accidentally cutting you off in the middle.

gateway   Technical Term   *Noun*

An entity that lets data travel between two very different parts of a network. An office might have a computer that acts as a gateway between the Internet and the local network of a half-dozen PC's. CompuServe and America Online have gateways that allow messages to be created on their services and then transmitted to the Internet. There are even snail-mail gateways, which allow messages to be printed out and physically mailed the old-fashioned way, which shows a laudable extreme of obfuscation of a basic task, something which quite frankly ought to be encouraged in this day and age.

gd&r   Online Style   *Interjection*

See Instead: **grin**

gearhead   Online Jargon   *Noun*

Complimentary term referring to a hacker who's obsessed with automobiles or mechanical engineering.

Geek Code   Online Jargon   *Noun*

Oh, sure, we all know you're a geek…but what kind of a geek are you? How well do you know UNIX? Do you never eat anything which isn't cocooned in cellophane? Any tattoos of Sun Microsystems' logo anywhere on your body?

To avoid the tedious and inefficient process known as "conversing," Robert Hayden developed and published a standardized system of code which allows you to codify your entire physical, intellectual, and psychic corpus in convenient 7-bit ASCII symbols. A small section of my own Geek Code is reproduced and annotated herein:

```
w----OM++++$VPS+PE
```

Translation: "I truly believe that Windows is something which God put upon His Earth to revenge himself upon Mankind for our having invented things like Styrofoam and Disco; have tried OS/2; sit at the right hand of Zeus as far as Macintosh knowledge is concerned, and furthermore exploit this status for cash on a regular basis; have used VMS; politically-speaking, believe that both parties are equally nuts; and more or less distrust both government and business."

The Geek Code is updated on a semi-regular basis and is available from dozens of online sources. The "official" source for it is http://krypton.mankato.msus .edu/~ hayden/geek.html.

GEnie   Online Entity   *Noun*

General Electric's entry in the marketplace of commercial online services. Originally was a low-cost alternative to CompuServe, and became quite successful on that basis, but the service failed to keep current with its competitors (offering graphical client software, Internet access, attracting new and unique services, etc.) and so became marginalized by AOL and CompuServe.

GIF   Technical Term   Noun

Graphics Interchange Format. Along with JPEG, one of
the two standard bitmapped graphics file formats used
by the Web. A GIF file will usually be much larger than
an identical JPEG, and unlike JPEG you're limited to a
palette of 256 colors, but the resulting image tends to
be noticeably sharper. Therefore, most webmasters
use the JPEG format with photographic images and
GIFs for artwork, particularly computer-generated
stuff. Pronounced with a hard "g."

glitch   Technical Term   *Noun*

See *Instead:* **bug**

gold   Technical Term   *Adjective*

Describes the status of a project, usually a piece of
software under development. When software has
"gone gold," that means the publisher has discovered
and fixed all of the bugs it thinks it can find and has
decided which "build" of the software package will be
released as the final product. It has often been said
that Microsoft goes straight from Alpha to Gold. This is
undoubtedly mere vicious rumor, but it answers a lot
of questions nonetheless. *See Also:* **alpha, beta**

golden   Online Jargon   *Adjective*

In pretty dashed fine shape. "Just download the updat-

ed version of that program, and you'll be golden"
means that you'll be rid of that nasty problem you
talked about.

gopher   Product   *Noun*

One of the predecessors of the World Wide Web. A
"Gopher site" presents a series of text-based menus
linked to files available for public access on an Internet
site. Still found on the Net, but almost completely
obsolete.

goth   Online Jargon   *Noun/ Adjective*

Short for gothic. Someone who dresses in black, reads
a lot of Neil Gaiman and Ann Rice, owns a skull in
addition to the one they had installed at the factory,
and whose lifestyle requires a lot of candles and dark,
heavy poetry.

.gov   Online Entity   *Noun*

See *Instead:* **domain**

green card   Online Jargon   *Noun/Adjective*

Derisive descriptive modifier, lofted at folks who bla-
tantly waste public bandwidth by posting fly-by-night
commercial schemes. Entered into the vernacular after

the classic such scheme, a spam inflicted upon the
Internet by a law firm advertising their immigration
services.

Example	Hey, take this green-card trash outside and leave it there, or risk finally receiving the brutal pummelling you've deserved since birth!!!

grid   Online Jargon   *Noun*

The whole of the communications systems. Whereas
the Net refers to the wide system of computers able
to share data, the Grid also includes phones, newspapers,
television…the entire global infrastructure for offload-
ing information into your brain. When you say you're
going to "unplug from the Net" for a little while, you're
just taking a little vacation from the crush of E-mail
and the Web and so forth. "Unplugging from the Grid"
means that Kathie Lee Gifford commercials and Jim
Carrey movies and tobacco billboards have finally sick-
ened you to the point where you're contacting mon-
asteries and asking to see their promotional videos.

grin   Online Style   *Interjection*

A method of conveying your emotions in a message.
Considered by many to be superior to emoticons
because (a) they're more dignified, and (b) the system
has no provision for negative emotions, of which we
already have more than enough, thank you very much.
Typically a grin is used either as an entire response to

a message that you found funny or appended to the end of your message to indicate that you're just kidding. Intensity of emotion can be conveyed two different ways. Classic use of a Grin is the form <g>, with multiple "g"'s indicating bigger smiles (as in <ggg>). The other method is to make up an acronym that includes the letter. The most popular acronyms of this type are:

<vbg> Very Big Grin

<gd&r> Grinning, ducking and running, in the manner of a vaudevillian who's just told an incredibly lame joke and is now dodging volleys of spoiled produce hurled by the audience.

See Also: **emoticons**

Example
> Well, of course you didn't get it. On the whole you've got the sense of humor of a pack of wet mice. <g>

grind (on)   Online Jargon   *Verb*

(of software) To work on a long and involved automated procedure.

Example
> My PowerMac is grinding on an 8M file transfer; don't worry, I've got at least fifteen minutes to talk.

grok   Online Jargon   *Verb*

To understand something so completely and so absolutely that you practically become the thing itself. "Can I help? I grok Word." means that this person knows Microsoft Word so well that he can even tell you what the programmer was eating when he wrote the word-wrap routine. From Robert Heinlein's *Stranger in a Strange Land.*

group   Online Entity   *Noun*

See *Instead:* **newsgroup**

guest   Technical Term   *Noun*

A special level of access that allows unregistered users to log in and use a system. Typically, the administrator of a system will define a special account so that if someone tries to log in under the username "guest," they will be allowed to enter the system without a password. Their activities will be severely limited, though; you can't have total strangers wreaking havoc on a system. (Of course, total strangers can log on as guests and wreak havoc, anyway, by exploiting holes in which might exist in the security system.)

GUI   Technical Term   *Noun*

Graphical User Interface. All of the onscreen doo-dads

like icons and windows and menus and such which let you have fun with your computer without having to mess around with a whole boatload of miserable, soul-sapping, inscrutable low-level commands. If I'm not actually writing a disparaging remark about the Microsoft Windows GUI here, I'm thinking one. Oh, you bet. *See Also:* **MacOS, Windows, OpenLook, Motif**

^H   Online Jargon   *Noun*

The control key which is the equivalent of hitting the "backspace" key. As a style thing, it's used to simulate the action of deleting something you've typed and re-placing it with something else. You can just imagine the big atomic laffs this can engender, in the right hands.

Example | "There's an easy explanation for why millions of users have made DiscoWriter the number one word processor for Windows: Payol^H^H^H^H^H Commitment to excellence."

hack   Online Jargon   *Noun/Verb*

To hack is to pursue a solution to a problem in a high-ly analog fashion (that is, by approaching things artisti-cally, rhythmically, intuitively, non-linearly, and above all doggedly) as opposed to a digital fashion (trusting in established and published data and procedures and pounding your fist on the keyboard when the pub-lished info proves to be overwhelmingly inadequate). Therefore, "I'm writing some C tonight" might be accurately interpreted to mean "My boss wants me to write a device driver for the new printer, so I'm going to just try modifying the old driver and the moment I get some sort of functioning code, I'm outta there!" If he says "I'm hacking some C tonight," then he's probably writing a program which will make anything you say into the computer's microphone come out sounding just like Barney Rubble. It is also likely that he got a 4000-line version of the program working three weeks ago, but is certain that he can get it down under 1000.

As a noun, any palpably nifty trick, usually some sort of technical solution. For instance, on many computers there's a hack for boosting the machine's speed by twenty to fifty percent by soldering a commonly-available five-dollar component onto the motherboard. A Hack can also be completely nontechnical; at MIT, there's the time-honored hack of hoisting an improbable object to the top of its main building's Great Dome.

hacker   Online Jargon   *Noun*

A term which has been abused and completely ruined by idiots in the mainstream media, man.

Strictly speaking, a hacker is a person whose curiosity about a subject (usually a technical one) is so intense that they're willing to go to great lengths to acquire as much knowledge about it as they can, even if it's unavailable from "official" sources. For example, consider those keyless door locks found in in some offices, which feature five pushbuttons and a doorknob. Most people look at them and wonder how secure they are. Most of those people would at best call the manufacturer and believe the official-ish numbers dictated to them about how many possible combinations there are.

A Hacker, on the other hand, would spend hours taking apart the lock in their office and examining the works. They'd physically test every weakness they could possibly imagine, and at the end of a week would discover either (a) that dang, these locks really are secure, or (b) a method by which they can open any five-button lock in the building in under ten minutes with absolutely no preparation.

And OK, admittedly a true hacker would indeed be giggling inwardly every second of every day afterward, because they know that if they really wanted to, they could break into absolutely any office they wanted to.

Traditionally, "hacker" is a compliment. Unfortunately, those losers in nameless magazines decided that "hacker" refers to people who break into computer systems and cause mayhem, and that's the definition which has stuck.

A personal aside: if you've derived any enjoyment at all out of this book, do me a favor. There was this absolutely idiotic movie released in 1995 called Hackers. I can't remember ever having a worse time in a theater. So if you find yourself in Blockbuster and you pass by that flick, and there's a good crowd of people, grab the title off the shelf and shout "HACK-ERS?!? What a total earwig of a movie! Geez, what idiot bought three copies of this for the store?!" and storm out. Somehow, somewhere, I'll know you've done it and will be grateful.

hacksploitation film

Online Jargon   *Noun*

A really, really bad movie about hackers. In a hacksploitation film, the hackers all have haircuts that cost more than a real hacker's entire wardrobe, impress each other with incredibly complicated technical "jargon" such as "Internet" and "RAM," and are able to "hack into" any object, such as a dish of Hershey's Kisses, that happens to be located in a room with a phone jack somewhere in it. Imagine all of those episodes of "The Lucy Show" in which Lucille Ball and Gayle Gordon dressed up as young people and went to "hippie freak-outs," and you will understand the full horror of the hacksploitation film. The ultimate hacksploitation film is, coincidentally, the 1995 release *Hackers*. The 1995 Sandra Bullock techno-thriller *The Net* is not a hacksploitation film; it was actually a pretty hip film, and besides, we like Sandra Bullock. She seems like a rather good egg and we like to think that we'd actually get on rather well if we met socially. You know, start an e-mail relationship, then maybe have lunch sometime when she's in town promoting her latest movie, and then phone calls and who knows? So I wish to stress that *The Net* is indeed a rather sharp movie and not the sort of rubbish the producers of *Hackers* decided to slap together, and that my e-mail address is andyi@world.std.com.

hakspek   Online Jargon   *Noun*

....

The very practical style of typing with as few characters as possible so to eke as much speed as possible from limited-bandwidth connections. Ppl uzd 2 tlk lyk ths bk wen ty nly hd 300 bps mdms & wr chtng lyv, but in this day and age hakspek is only used by people who saw it in a hacksploitation film and thought it looked cool. *See Also:* **leeguage**

half duplex   Technical Term   *Noun/Verb*

Sort of an antiquated term for communications which
can only go in one direction at a time. A walkie-talkie,
for instance, is half-duplex; you can only have a conversation with someone if you take turns talking. With
rare exception, all modem communication today is
full-duplex, meaning data can be transmitted at both
ends of the connection simultaneously.

handle   Online Jargon   *Noun*

One of the many enduring legacies of that rich CB
Radio culture, a handle is simply a name (more like a
persona, really) you use online rather than disclosing
what's there on your driver's license. There's no hard
and fast rules about the usage of handles. On IRC, for
instance, handles are the customary means of identity.
On the other hand, many online forums (like some on
commercial services) actively discourage their use. *See
Also:* **screen name**

hang   Online Jargon   *Noun*

See Instead: **freeze**

Hanlon's Razor   Online Jargon   *Noun*

"Never attribute to malice what can be adequately
explained by stupidity." Insanely popular quote, also

handy in that it sheds some light on 90% of what you might read on Usenet.

hard-wrapped   Technical Term   *Adjective*

Of a text file, having carriage-return symbols at the end of every line. This concept used to be a godsend in the olden days of the Eighties, when it allowed text files to display properly on old-fashioned terminal software and word processors (which used monospaced fonts), but nowadays it's a nuisance; if your window isn't sized properly, these physical carriage returns cause lines to break in wacky ways. Also, those carriage returns have to be stripped out before the text can be used in a modern word processor.

hardwired   Online Jargon   *Adjective*

A feature which is physically burned in and cannot be removed or even overridden. Of specific people, a fundamental nature which can never be overcome.

Hawaiian Punch   Product   *Noun*

See *Instead:* **Jolt Cola**

header   Technical Term   *Noun*

Generic term for data that appears at the very beginning of a sequence of data. In communications parlance, it refers to the block of information at the beginning of a message that describes who sent it, when, and how. Most mailreaders hide this information from you unless you specifically ask to see it; it's fairly gnarly-looking and of little practical use.

heavy iron   Online Jargon   *Noun*

A computer too large and heavy to throw, like a mainframe or a minicomputer or the original Apple Macintosh Portable.

hir   Online Jargon   *Pronoun*

Him or Her; He or She; a gender-neutral third-person pronoun. It's awfully tedious to keep writing these over and over again in a message, so forward-thinking netters who want to nonetheless stave off the ol' carpal-tunnel syndrome will write things like ''Any programmer worth hir salt knows that Hawaiian Punch is the best system for delivering the most sugar and caffeine within the shortest amount of time.''

hit   Technical Term   *Noun*

The popularity of a website is generally gauged by the number of ''hits'' it generates—the number of times a file on that site is accessed by a user. Technically, though, this is misleading; if a webpage contains five graphics, then accessing the page generates six ''hits'' (one for the HTML document itself and one for each of the graphics files), so people count page requests instead. The lack of a simple, reliable way to determine a website's popularity is an ongoing source of frustration to the members of the industrial bourgeoisie who want to fully exploit the Web's commercial potential. After all, how can you convince a cigarette company to advertise on your site unless you can prove you get more visits from nonsmokers ages 8–18 than your competitors?

homepage   Online Jargon   *Noun*

Used almost interchangeably with "website," (as in "check out my homepage sometime") though it also refers to the "default" page, which a webserver transmits when a browser doesn't specify which page of a website it wants. This corresponds to the "top" or "main page" of the website.

hosed   Online Jargon   *Adjective*

Damaged in an exceptionally messy way, though not necessarily beyond repair. Generally indicates that one piece of software screwed up and damaged another piece of software, for unknown reasons. *See Also:* **thrashed, throcked, trashed**

Example | Hey, that download got hosed on the server. Could you post it again?

host   Technical Term   *Noun*

Means more or less what it means in the real world.
You go to a party, the host's house is your house,
and if you get drinks and food, it's because the host
serves it to you. Similarly, when you dial into a host
computer, you're using its services for as long as
you're connected, though you're not technically a
part of that computer.

hotel   Online Jargon   *Noun*

A system of lodgings where seasoned netizens go when
they want to get away from the hustle and bustle of
the online world. Toward that end, helpful hotel managers have installed a special in-house phone system
that uses a proprietary dial tone unrecognizable by
any standard modem, operates on line voltages that
will fry all telcom equipment but their own Soviet-
made hotel phones, and operates on largely hydraulic
principles. On the off chance that a guest would like
to retrieve his e-mail from his room, the proprietor is
usually willing to unscrew a hatch over hidden port in
the floor, allowing access to a standard phone line for
a nominal charge of a hundred dollars a night.

hotlist   Online Jargon   *Noun*

A list of all of one's favorite URLs. It's quite common
for folks to publish their hotlists on their websites.
Indeed, hotlists usually offer links to the very swellest
sites.

hot-swappable   Technical Term   *Adjective*

Of a hardware accessory, a design which allows you to install or remove it without needing to shut down the computer first. Most expansion cards (like PCI cards) would fry the computer and/or you if you tried to take it out without turning the machine off first. For many accessories, like modems, storage devices, etc., this isn't terribly convenient, and so they're specifically designed to be removed and inserted at will. Note that devices have to be designed with this in mind: a PC Card-based modem can be popped out at any time, but if you try to remove your PCI-based modem card from your desktop PC before you turn it off, you might very well get the opportunity to tell Abe Lincoln how the second half of Our American Cousin turned out.

.hqx   Technical Term   *Noun*

File extension for a file encoded in the BinHex file format.

HTML   Technical Term   *Noun*

Hyper-Text Markup Language. A form of SGML, HTML consists of dozens of standard "tags" that tell a web browser how a certain item (text, pictures, etc) is to be displayed when the document is read. HTML is not a programming language per se; it's more like a set of "cues" for the browser to follow. For instance, if this line is in an HTML document, "I've seen <i>Star

Wars</i> 98 times!" the browser knows that "Stars Wars" is to be displayed in italics. All HTML appears in pointy brackets surrounding the item to be affected. *See Also:* **tag**

.html   Technical Term   *Noun*

File extension for a file tagged in HTML.

http   Technical Term   *Noun*

Hyper-Text Transfer Protocol. The protocol by which your web browser and a web server communicate with each other. When a URL begins with "http," it indicates that the URL points to a webpage, as opposed to, say, a telnet address.

IAB   Organization   *Noun*

Internet Architecture Board. What the American Medical Association is to health, the IAB is to the Internet. They basically decide what's best for the Net, now and for the future.

IDEA   Specification   *Noun*

International Data Encryption Algorithm. A brain-bangingly secure encryption algorithm incorporated as part of PGP. Monumentally faster and more secure than DES or RSA.

IEEE   Organization   *Noun*

Institute of Electrical and Electronics Engineers. International organization which develops and maintains standards related to networking and electronics. Sometimes used colloquially as an adjective, as in "I think five twelve-packs of Coke Classic is part of the IEEE specification for lab refrigerator contents or something…"

IMAP   Technical Term   *Noun*

See *Instead:* **image map**

image map   Technical Term   *Noun*

A graphic image on a website which, when clicked, can send you to any one of a number of different URLs. Which URL depends on where in the image you clicked. The classic example of an image map is a map of the United States in which clicking on a state will take you to the webpage of that state's capitol.

IMHO   Online Jargon   *Noun*

In My Humble Opinion. A proper sign of humility

when you're about to, nevertheless, tell someone that their last statement was a complete load of dingo's kidneys.

IMO   Online Jargon   *Noun*

In My Opinion. An even less humble version of IMHO.

Infoseek   Online Entity   *Noun*

Internet search engine found at http://guide.infoseek.com/. Combines the nicest features of AltaVista and Yahoo.

insanely   Online Jargon   *Suffix/Modifier*

Unbelievably. Used exclusively in a positive way.

Intel   Organization   *Noun*

Company which makes the CPUs that almost all Windows-based machines use. Therefore, colloquially used to refer to any machine that runs Windows.

Example | `I've got an Intel machine.`

intellectual property

Technical Term   *Noun*

....

Catch-all legal term referring to creative works, such as writings, music, software, symbols, etc. "Intellectual property rights" refers to things like your right to put your database of Beatles cover songs on your webpage, and restrict other people from copying it and publishing that data for their own profit.

interlaced GIF   Technical Term   *Noun*

....

A flavor of the GIF format in which the picture data isn't stored and retrieved in a strictly top-to-bottom order. This is seen in the "venetian blind" visual effect you get when an interlaced GIF is read onto the screen. In certain web browsers (like Netscape) an additional visual effect is applied to interlaced GIFs so that the picture appears to "come into focus" gradually.

internet computer   Product   *Noun*

....

A generic term for a cheap ($500 or less) computer which plugs into your TV set and brings Internet services (mail, shopping, websurfing) into the home. Literally all of the major players in the industry have their own working prototypes for these mass-market devices, and hope that they'll become the Nintendo of the Nineties. No one wants to be the first to start mass-producing them, though, as the market for them is rather dodgy; those who are genuinely interested in the Internet are generally willing to pay more for a full computer system, and even the $500 price tag might prove too hefty for people who could care less about the World Wide Web.

Internet Config   Product   *Noun*

Freeware utility for Macintosh that maintains a standardized central database in your system folder of Internet configuration para-meters (such as your username, the name of your ISP, signature files, etc.). This allows Internet software to automatically install and configure itself, provided it was programmed to take advantage of Internet Config's database.

Internet Proper   Online Jargon   *Noun*

The Internet Proper is a term that hardcore longtime Internet users (like myself) began to adopt when America Online and CompuServe allowed even those people who can't set the clocks on their VCRs to access websites, newsgroups, and fileservers. The Internet Proper is that part of the Internet that is not found exclusively on CIS or AOL or any other commercial service. To say that you have a Proper Internet Connection means that your ISP is a local host system and not CompuServe or America Online. OK, sure, it's elitist and self-serving, but those are two of the legs on that wonderful five-legged stool we call the "Computer Culture."

internet telephone   Product   *Noun*

Any one of many different TCP-based software products which allows you to use the Internet as a long-
distance carrier. You got a computer and a modem,
right? These two things work together to send digital
information over a phone line, right? And you also
have either a Macintosh or a Windows box with multimedia, which can record sound over a microphone
and convert it to digital information. The software just
acts as the glue between you, the person you want to
call, the Internet, and all of that hardware, and the
upshot is that if you're paying your ISP $20 a month
for unlimited access, the cost of a 189-hour phone call
from Boston to New Delhi will be absolutely zero.
Obviously, this has the collective underwear of the
telephone industry in a knot, and they're fiercely lob-
bying The Gummint to declare makers of this software
to be Long-Distance Carriers and therefore subject to
federal communications regulations.

InterNIC   Organization   *Noun*

The organization responsible for registering Internet
domain names and maintaining the DNS database.

intranet   Technical Term   *Noun*

A system of Internet-type resources that are not actually part of the Internet per se. A private company's

in-house computer network might have its own web-server and its own public and private mail systems, and they might even use exactly the same software as you use. However, this system is not open to the public—hey, it might not even have any links to the outside world at all—which means it's an intranet and not part of the Internet. File this under "Buzzwords."

IOW   Online Jargon   *Interjection*

In Other Words.

IP   Technical Term   *Noun*

Internet Protocol. The low low low low LOW (I'm talking really low-level) communications protocol used on the Internet. You know how, at its lowest level, a human conversation exists as a sequence of pulsed changes in air pressure? That's IP's relationship with digital communications. Please just accept my "low low (etc.)" definition and save both of us a great deal of time and pages of text. Think of the trees, I beg you!

IPng   Technical Term   *Noun*

Internet Protocol: The Next Generation. With everyone demanding an IP address for every device in their office all the way down to the coffeemaker, there's the concern that soon the Internet is going to run out of IP addresses. IPng is an enhanced IP which supports more addresses, as well as a bunch of other built-in features to make the Net easier and more secure.

IPX   Technical Term   *Noun*

Novell's networking protocol, most popularly used in Novel NetWare.

IRC   Technical Term   *Noun*

Internet Relay Chat. Sort of a cross between live online conferencing and CB radio for the Internet. Once you've installed IRC software on your machine, you can connect to an IRC server and jump into a specific IRC channel. Each channel name begins with a "#" and is dedicated to a different area of interest. Channels are always open, but generally there are regularly scheduled "meetings" in which people specifically gather to talk.

IrDA   Technical Term   *Noun*

InfraRed Data Association. A scheme for allowing hardware to communicate via infrared light (the same way your TV remote communicates with your TV). Potentially a very cool concept, if every hardware manufacturer embraces it. At a boardroom meeting where you and your friend are sitting across the table from each other with your notebook PCs, you can silently send each other messages about what a dork the chairman is, without the need for messy cables.

IRQ   Technical Term   *Noun*

....

Interrupt Request. In Wintel architecture, the CPU
maintains a specific limited number of open data
lines (IRQs) to certain peripherals so that they can
grab the processor's attention immediately if they
have to, for instance, so the serial port can keep
shoveling in data from the modem without losing
any. Typical devices that would use a hardware IRQ
would be communications cards (like Ethernet
adapters), sound boards, SCSI interfaces, and the
like. This system can cause endless headaches
because each IRQ interrupt has to have its own
unique ID, so if you take home that nice new flatbed
scanner and install its interface card, you might find
that the software to run it simply won't work
 because its default IRQ is already taken by another
peripheral. That means you have to get out the book
and assign it a new one, and unless you're good at
keeping track of arcane information you might have
to wind up taking some educated guesses. When a
Mac-versus-Windows debate has entered its third
hour and tempers are beginning to flare, the Macintosh proponent will draw the argument to a quick
and cruel conclusion by drawing close to that poor
Windows slob and plainly saying "Oh? Say, last weekend I bought a video capture board for my Power-
Mac. Just plugged it into one of the slots and bango,
the sucker worked straight away. And how is that
back-up drive you bought two months ago? Working
yet, is it?" And at that point the Windows fellow pales
and slinks off to get another drink.

ISDN   Technical Term   *Noun*

Integrated Services Digital Network. ISDN is to current copper wire phone lines what Steven Spielberg's computer-generated dinosaurs are to Bert I. Gordon's iguanas with fins glued onto them. An ISDN line offers multiple channels (that is, you can have your Internet connection, your phone line, cable TV, and delivery of hot, fresh pizza simultaneously over the same fiber-optic ISDN cable) and brain-banging speed (typically, you get multiple channels of 64kbps). Your local phone company does have to offer ISDN service, of course, plus you'll need special equipment (ISDN modems, etc), but man alive, being an adult with an ISDN line at the house is like being a kid with an in-ground pool. The respect you get from your little playmates is pretty dashed formidable.

ISO   Organization   *Noun*

International Standardization Organization. Another one of those international aggregations of engineers who get together every now and then to pad out their corporate expense accounts at the hotel bar and incidentally figure out how to get the Bündespost to interface nicely with British Telcom.

ISO 9000   Technical Term   *Noun*

International procedures for quality control. It pops up in "Dilbert" every week or so. It is correct to say that

ISO 9000 has not impressed Dilbert's creator as a magic cure-all for problems of planning, production, and distribution.

ISP   Technical Term   *Noun*

Internet Service Provider. The organization that provides you with access to the Internet.

JAM   Online Jargon   *Interjection*

Just A Minute.

Java   Product   *Noun*

Sun Microsystem's programming language for the Internet. Whereas HTML is just a mark-up language that describes which bits of a document are links and which bits should be rendered in boldface, and CGI scripts allow a webserver to create content-on-demand for webpages, Java allows a programmer full control of a section of real estate in a Java-capable web-browser; with few limitations, any software you can write for a personal computer can be written in Java. The upshot is that Java allows a level of intimacy and interactivity previously unheard of on the Web. Instead of a static webpage not much different from a paper printout, the user literally is working with a piece of interactive software, just as though they'd installed it from a disk. A programmer creates "applets" in the JavaScript language and then places the applets and their webpages on their website. The webpage is standard HTML, except it specifies a bit of square acreage which will be controlled by a Java applet. One of the many cool things about Java is that these applets are platform-independent; the programmer doesn't have to write one version for Macs, another for Windows, a third for Unix, etc. These applets don't even necessarily have to be run over the Net. Indeed, several software publishers are investigating the feasibility of releasing their products as Universal Java applets instead of producing a different version for each operating system. Depending on whom you ask, Java will either bring about a new era of peace and international unity, or else the "Industry" will give up on it after it fails to figure out how to make a buck on it. Sort of a toss-up at this point.

JavaScript   Technical Term   *Noun*

The programming language used to write Java applets.

Jolt Cola   Product   *Noun*

Awful-tasting beverage hypersaturated with sugar and caffeine. Somewhat legendary as the "hacker drink" for helping people stay up later and later, but that's more of an urban legend. Most hackers either can stay awake on their own, or they choose a superior delivery system, such as Mello-Yello (shockingly high caffeine and pleasant taste) or Hawaiian Punch (enormous amount of sugar, plus the fact that it's not carbonated means you can slam down a 96-ounce dose in under thirty seconds and then get on with your work).

JPEG   Technical Term   *Noun*

Joint Photographic Experts Group. Self-explanatory, eh? Alright, JPEG is a scheme for compressing images and the term is also used for the file format of a JPEG-compressed image. Along with GIF, it's the ubiquitous graphics format of the Internet. Unlike GIF, it can produce truly astonishing levels of compression, and is flexible enough to encode pictures millions of colors deep. Also unlike GIF, it's a "lossy" scheme in which the more tightly an image is compressed, the coarser the resulting image will appear when decompressed. As a result, JPEG is usually used for compressing photographs, in which the strict loss of a pixel here or there isn't terribly noticeable. *See Also:* **GIF**

.JPG   Technical Term   *Noun*

File extension for the JPEG graphical file format.

Kermit   Technical Term   *Noun/Verb*

An outdated file-transfer protocol developed at

Columbia University. It was all the rage up to the mid-Eighties or so, but then was replaced by more agile protocols. It's still supported by many comm programs, chiefly because it's more trouble to remove the code than to just leave it in there. Yes, it was named after the avuncular amphibian, with permission.

killfile Technical Term *Noun*

So, have you ever tried to get into one of those fancy parties where there's a beefy guy at the door with a list of names, and if your name isn't on the list, you can't get in? A killfile is that list in reverse. If a person's address is in your killfile, then your news or mailreader—assuming it supports killfiles—will pretend that all messages or postings from that address don't exist. If someone's been sending you harrassing mail, or if there's this one bozo on your favorite newsgroup who keeps flaming everyone, just toss his address in the killfile and, poof, it's as though he never existed.

Example | Ed, it seems like your address and my killfile were destined to get together sooner or later. Goodbye.

KISS Online Jargon *Noun*

Keep It Simple, Stupid. An admonition, as well as a design philosophy which states that the fewer features something has, the better it runs.

kluge   Online Jargon   *Noun*

A sloppy and inelegant solution that, nonetheless, works. As a verb, to solve a problem by a kluge. *See Also:* **quick-and-dirty**

koan   Online Jargon   *Noun*

In Zen terminology, a koan is a riddle between a priest and his dim-witted student, which when recounted to another dim-witted pupil leads to big-time illumination. Therefore, Internet koans (and programming koans, and end-user koans) are popular among experienced Netters.

lamer   Online Jargon   *Noun*

A newbie lacking the interest or ambition to improve his or her station. A new user who tries to reads a book about the Internet (or more likely, an article in a technical publication like *People*), gets an America Online account, and tries to pass himself off as Mr. Legion-Of-Doom-Superhacker in public forums, using impossibly contrived jargon to comical effect. Shoddily produced mass-market "cyber-lingo" type dictionaries are the most common contributor to the lamer problem.

LAN   Technical Term   *Noun*

Local Area Network. A network of computers in a relatively small area, like inside one building. As you might guess by this definition, the term is a rather subjective one, and is simply used to draw a distinction between a simple network for letting workers print files and exchange mail with each other, and a Wide Area Network, which links the Boston office with the Dallas, Wichita, and Boca Raton offices as well as allowing satellite links from salesmen in the field. *See Also:* **WAN**

LAPM   Technical Term   *Noun*

Link Access Procedure for Modems, a method of error-checking included in the V.42 standard.

latency   Technical Term   *Noun*

The "big if" in the speed equation. In any transfer of data (live concert video from a webcast, just to choose an example) you just can't predict how much time is going to elapse between the moment the "broadcasting" computer squirts the first guitar chord into the Internet to the moment some shmo's modem actually receives it. Therefore, folks who have billions of dollars riding on America's desire to pay $79 to see the Internet-only broadcast of the Super Bowl are scared green by the concept of latency and work hard to keep the Internet's latency to the shortest interval possible.

leased line   Technical Term   *Noun*

As opposed to a dial-up connection, a special line

which connects you and your host directly.

LEC   Technical Term   *Noun*

Local Exchange Carrier. The company which gives you phone service. Usually owned by one of the Baby Bells.

leeguage   Online Jargon   *Noun*

Affected, embarrassing, and tiresome vogue of using misspelled words and made-up jargon to conform to a perceived "hacker chic." Rules vary from individual to individual, but mainstays include substituting "Z" for "S" and numbers for similar-sounding parts of words. Originally named in honor of Pamela Anderson Lee's bosom, which, like this language, is completely un-natural, constructed with tortuous effort, and con-forms to some vaguely perceived standard no one comprehends.

Example | Hay! Odz r he wen 2 Radio Hack 4 a
             nu crys 4 hiz rainbo boxx!

line noise   Technical Term   *Noun*

The static, hissing, intercepted AM radio broadcasts, etc. on a phone line that interfere with communica-tions. This used to be a real bother, but now that almost all modems have sophisticated error-checking

protocols built-in, it's usually no more than a minor
nuisance.

link   Technical Term   *Noun/Verb*

A URL embedded in a webpage that takes you to
another webpage (or Internet resource) when clicked.
Your browser will highlight all of the links on a page
(usually by underlining them and drawing them in a
different color) to call your attention to them.

Linux   Product   *Noun*

An implementation of UNIX released as freeware
for a multitude of hardware platforms. Has taken
root in the Internet culture as the power operating
system of choice. Macintosh versus Windows debates
rage on and on, but many folks feel that by jumping
in and declaring that they use Linux, they render all
debate moot.

list   Online Jargon   *Noun*

A mailing list.

list server   Online Entity   *Noun*

A program that controls a mailing list. It processes
online requests from people who wish to join a spe-

cific mailing list and distributes mail to the list. This is fully automated. Merely sending an e-mail message to the right list server with a keyword in its "Subject" line adds your address to the list.

Listserv   Product   *Noun*

A specific list server.

LocalTalk   Technical Term   *Noun*

The Apple networking protocol that ships with all Macintoshes. LocalTalk works over one of the Mac's RS-422 serial ports and as such is far, far slower than Ethernet. On the bright side, it costs about ten bucks to fit a Mac with a LocalTalk connector (versus $60 or more for an Ethernet transciever) and individual machines can be connected up with standard phone cord. First known as AppleTalk, before Apple got all keen on promoting it as a multi-platform standard.

log in, log on   Technical Term   *Noun*

To pass an online entity's security screening (by typing in a recognized userid and a password) and establish a connection. Refers to the fact that the machine won't allow you inside until it has made a note of your identity and the time on its userlog.

LOL   Online Jargon   *Interjection*

Laughing Out Loud. Sent as a response to a post that the reader found very funny indeed.

lose   Online Jargon   *Noun*

Something that doesn't work or fails to work in a particularly spectacular fashion. Myriad variants of this term exist—lossage, lossity, Big Lose, etc.

lossy   Technical Term   *Adjective*

Descriptive of a data-compression scheme where in order to scrunch the data down as tightly as possible, some data will be lost. A "lossy" algorithm (such as JPEG) therefore can't possibly be used to compress a piece of software—if even one bit is mislaid, the program just won't run—but it's just fine when it comes to compressing pictures, video, or sound. It's sort of like writing "Mass." instead of "Massachusetts." Not all of the original data is there, but enough is there that we can see the original intent.

lurker   Online Jargon   *Noun*

Someone who frequents an online public forum (message base, conference, etc.) but does not actively participate (one who reads messages but does not post.) Lurking is a vital part of the development process if you want to become a full-fledged member of the online community. By spending a few weeks simply lurking in a newsgroup and resisting the impulse to post replies, you'll learn the unwritten rules of etiquette without forcing someone to point them out to you personally via some unsettlingly direct threats involving a red-hot ice cream scooper. It also helps you avoid newbie social blunders like unknowingly telling a newsgroup's very own tenured professor of English literature that he's probably never even read *Jane Eyre* and that arrogant high school kids like him shouldn't pretend to know more than they actually do.

luser   Online Jargon   *Noun*

Combination of loser and user. It's possible to respect and, even in rare exceptions, to actually befriend those who use the software which you either write or support; but when a user calls you complaining that his computer keeps telling him to "Press any key" and he can't find a single one marked "any," he becomes a luser.

Lycos   Online Jargon   *Noun*

Popular Internet search engine, found at http://www.lycos.com/.

lynx   Product   *Noun*

A text-only World Wide Web browser, popular

among those who access the Internet through shell accounts. Also popular among the visually impaired.

LZW   Technical Term   *Noun*

Lempel-Ziv-Welch. A ridiculously ubiquitous algorithm for compressing data. Chances are, right now you've got at least five pieces of software that use it in some fashion. GIF graphics are compressed with LZW, as are most data compression products, as does the v.42bis modem standard, as does...

MacBinary   Technical Term   *Noun*

A special format for transmogrifying the unique structure of a Macintosh file into a form that can be handled by any operating system. Specifically, the file's resource and data forks are melded together, and its filename and attributes are encoded and stored so that the file can be reconstructed when it makes it way back to the MacOS.

Mach   Product   *Noun*

Version of UNIX developed at Carnegie-Mellon that serves as the common "open" specification of UNIX. With some exceptions, most of the commercially available and freely distributable UNIXs are different flavors of Mach.

Macıntosh   Product   *Noun*

Formerly specific and now generic term for a computer which exclusively runs the Macintosh operating system.

Macıntrash   Online Jargon   *Noun*

Derisive term for "Macintosh." The appearance of this word in a message subject line means that a monumental flame war is about to begin and if you have any sense, you'll opt to spend the next few weeks just reading some good books.

MacOS   Technical Term   *Noun*

The technically correct term for the Macintosh GUI and operating system. Apple started using this term when they finally, finally decided that it would actually be a pretty cool thing to have the Macintosh operating system running on machines not manufactured by Apple. "Cool Thing" used here as a euphemism for "way to keep Apple stockholders from voting to turn the whole company into a psychic pals hotline."

macro   Technical Term   *Noun*

A short sequence of keystrokes or commands you've defined that your software automatically expands into a longer and more complicated one. Typing "/close" in your word processor can be a macro for a paragraph-long closing to a business letter.

MacTCP   Product   *Noun*

Apple's TCP stack for the Macintosh. Obsoleted with the introduction of Open Transport, but still used on older Macs.

Magellan   Online Entity   *Noun*

Internet search engine at http://www.mckinley.com/. Reviews many websites on a five-point scale.

mail bomb   Technical Term   *Noun*

An e-mail message with an enormous binary file included, sent with the hopes that it will crash the recipient's mailserver or mailreader. Pretty dashed anti-social.

mailbot   Technical Term   *Noun*

A piece of software that automatically initiates some sort of mail action without your direct command. Oftentimes programmers who go off for a vacation will leave a mailbot running that replies to every message received with some canned text telling the sender they won't get a response for two weeks.

mailing list   Technical Term   *Noun*

(1) Just like in the real world, a group of addresses that conceptually act as one. Most mail software allows you to define mailing lists, so that you can send a layoff notice to a list you've defined and named "THE COMPANY," instead of sending out 4,000 individual pieces of e-mail. Because under those circumstances, I mean, your time is probably better spent investing your $500,000 golden parachute.

(2) A discussion group whose messages are distributed through e-mail. Mailing lists are run by list servers.

mailreader   Technical Term   *Noun*

Software (either on your desktop computer or on your ISP) which allows you to read and reply to e-mail.

mailserver   Technical Term   *Noun*

See *Instead:* **server**

mainframe   Technical Term   *Noun*

Objects of hours of nostalgia. Mainframes are enormous behemoth computers that take up the entire floor of an office building and operate at such high temperatures that they often act as the central heat-ing system of the building they're installed in (true). Used to great cinematic effect in the classic Tracy/ Hepburn film *Desk Set* and the brilliant Don Knotts classic *How To Frame A Figg*. *See Also:* **heavy iron**

man page   Online Jargon   *Noun*

On UNIX systems, the entire mountainous pile of documentation for the system and all of its commands are available online. If you know that the newsreader "nn" had a feature for looking for postings from a spe-cific person but can't remember how to use it, typing "man nn" at the UNIX prompt will bring it right up. In effect, a really big instruction manual for UNIX. Or, make up your own joke.

marilyn's curse   Online Jargon   *Noun*

Any posting whose only purpose is to smugly point out the spelling errors in another post is cursed to have misspellings of its own, no matter how carefully the poster types. The poster is then left wide open to hails of derision and shocking loss of self-esteem. Which is as it should be.

Mello - Yello   Product   *Noun*

See Instead: **Jolt Cola**

Microsoft   Company   *Noun*

Makers of Microsoft Windows and dashed near every other piece of software on the planet. The secret of Microsoft's runaway commercial success is a simple one. Take a look at everything that's popular in American culture today. You got hit movies based on Seventies sitcoms. The kids today are galavanting around in those bell-bottom pants and polyester shirts again, buying KISS and Village People albums on vinyl. Aaron Spelling is once again the top TV producer, with multiple retreads of his action and jiggle shows of the Seventies and Eighties. It all points to one conclusion: nostalgia sells. Microsoft is just one of many commercial concerns latching on to this trend, creating an operating system whose feature set and user interface take you back to the halcyon days of the Early Eighties. Oh, sure, those losers with Macintoshes are using state-of-the-art technologies, but Windows users are retro-hip, man.

Microsoft Internet Explorer

Product   *Noun*

Microsoft woke up, rubbed the sleep from its eyes, picked up the paper, shot out of bed, and hit its head on the ceiling. "Gorblimey!" it collectively shouted. "This here Internet is getting mighty popular! People are taking the money they were going to spend on Microsoft product upgrades and are spending it on the Internet instead!" And this certainly wouldn't do, as you can understand. And, seemingly, a week later, Microsoft released Internet Explorer, a damned fine (and free) web-browser, which has been the first browser to compete effectively with Netscape Navigator.

.mil　　Online Entity　　*Noun*

See Instead: **domain**

Milnet　　Technical Term　　*Noun*

A section of the Internet consisting of hardware run by the valiant men and women of the United States Armed Services. Buy war bonds where you work or bank!

MIME　　Technical Term　　*Noun*

Multipurpose Internet Mail Extension. This multi-platform standard was developed when it became clear that a simple and straightforward mechanism was needed for attaching files to mail messages. If your mail program supports this standard, it can examine special encoding in a piece of e-mail (or a Usenet posting), which describes what sort of file is attached and how your mail program should process it.

minitower　　Online Jargon　　*Noun*

A tower that is short enough to keep on top of your desk instead of under it.

MIPS   Technical Term   *Noun*

Millions of Instructions Per Second. A rather antiquated way to compare raw computing power of two machines. This speed test relied on out-of-date concepts of how computers are used and, as such, is no longer used as a reliable method of comparison.

mirror site   Technical Term   *Noun*

A site (usually an FTP site) whose sole purpose is to duplicate all of the data found on another specific site. Once a site becomes insanely popular (such as RTFM, the MIT FTP site for Usenet FAQs), it becomes exceedingly difficult to access. Into the breach jumps some sysop with space on his server who sets up scripts that keeps the data on the mirror site up-to-date with the data on the original and, as a result, accessing one is as good as accessing the other.

MNP   Technical Term   *Noun*

Microcom Networking Protocol. A series of protocols for specific modem features, usually found as part of a v. specification. Most commonly heard of is MNP 5, which was the popular standard for modem-level data compression before v.42 came along.

modem   Technical Term   *Noun*

Modulator-Demodulator. Third only to television and ineffective middle-management as an entity that keeps you from getting your work done on time.

MOO Technical Term *Noun*

MUD, Only with Objects. Adds the rock 'em, sock 'em excitement of pictures and sound to the MUD experience.

MORF Online Jargon *Noun*

Male Or Female? Usually used in live, one-to-one chat, it's a simple acronym that helps you figure out whether or not you should give in to that impulse to invite this stranger to a bar for gin and tonics.

morphing Online Jargon *Noun*

Hacking a message header so that it appears to have been sent by someone else. In concept and in practice it's like mailing a letter with an incorrect return address in the upper corner of the envelope; it can be trivially easy to do, so people who rely on the security of their mail should be aware. The only easy way to be certain of a sender's identity is to arrange for the sender to use some form of public-key encryption, such as PGP. *See Also:* **remailer, cloak**

Mosaic Product *Noun*

Freeware web-browser, available in versions for all

major platforms. Mosaic is the browser that really started it all, but the fact that it's failed to keep up with its competitors (Netscape Navigator and Microsoft Internet Explorer) means that it's been relegated to the status of Quaint Relic rather than Important Internet Power Tool.

MOTD   Technical Term   *Noun*

Message Of The Day. Like a fortune, it's a little funny saying that comes up on some systems automatically when you log in. Just the system administrator's way of turning your Monday-morning frown upside down. Sometimes the MOTD is used to announce system problems, social gatherings, and general stuff.

Motif   Product   *Noun*

The most popular GUI for UNIX machines, developed by the Open Software Foundation. Kind of looks like a classier version of Windows.

mount   Technical Term   *Verb*

To establish a connection to a remote volume over a network that, conceptually at least, allows you to work with that volume as if it were an internal hard drive. That is, instead of issuing file-transfer commands and using various protocols to move a file from your PC's hard drive to the remote volume, you could simply drag the file's icon from the hard-drive's folder into the remote volume's folder. More generically, it refers to the simple action of a volume presenting itself as ready, willing, and able to the computer it's physically installed on, e.g., "Dang! My PowerBook's hard drive won't mount!"

.mov   Technical Term   *Noun*

File extension for QuickTime movie files.

Mozilla   Online Entity   *Noun*

Netscape's mascot…that green Godzilla-type dinosaur who pops up from time to time on Netscape websites and documentation. Click in Netscape's "Destination" box and type "about:mozilla" for further illumination.

MPC   Technical Term   *Noun*

Multimedia PC. A Wintel industry standard for describing the multimedia capabilities of a certain PC, such as the type of processor, hard-disk capacity, CD-ROM speed, and sound and video capabilities. If that hot new game has "Requires MPC Level 2" stamped on the box, you can be sure that you won't be able to play it on that 12-year-old PC you fished out of the dumpster behind the state prison.

.mpg   Technical Term   *Noun*

File extension for MPEG movie file format.

MPEG   Technical Term   *Noun*

Motion Picture Experts Group. A format for compressing and storing digital video (and the name of the committee which defined it). MPEG consists (for the most part) of JPEG compression plus an algorithm that checks for pixels that don't change from one frame to the next one and therefore don't have to be re-written. MPEG is hot stuff because it's such a flexible standard. It can be used as a cheap way to squeeze a thumbnail-sized video window into a small amount of storage space or it can be used to encode video frames large enough and detailed enough to rival the quality of actual film. For even near-videotape quality, though, MPEG requires a special decompression chip.

MUD   Technical Term   *Noun*

Multi-User Dungeon. Alternatively, Multi-User Dimension. A sort of text-based live Internet conference geared toward the playing of online games.

multicast   Online Jargon   *Noun/Verb*

A generic term referring to a transfer of information

(usually something like live text, sound, or video) in which a small group of people are transmitting to a vastly larger group. Your basic, seems-to-happen-every-week Internet event wherein some has-been band performs a live number on their website is a classic example of a multicast.

multimedia   Online Jargon   *Noun*

The combination of any two sorts of media in one presentation. Text and pictures. Pictures and sound. Video and text. Pork and beans. Death and taxes. A term that has been so buzzworded to death that it's practically meaningless.

multitask   Online Jargon   *Verb*

In a technical sense, multitasking is the ability of an operating system to run more than one piece of software simultaneously. Conversationally, it means you're doing more than one thing at once. For instance, if someone heard clicking in the background while talking to me on the phone and asked if I were too busy to talk, I might say "Naw, don't worry…I'm just multitasking."

NAK   Online Jargon   *Noun*

The low-level signal one piece of comm equipment sends another to tell it that it didn't receive that last packet of information correctly and it should be resent. Used similarly in conversation, to mean "You're making no sense whatsoever; I must hit you now." *See Also:* **ACK**

nastygram   Online Jargon   *Noun*

Any awful piece of e-mail. Also used as a synonym for mailbomb.

NDA   Technical Term   *Noun*

See Instead: **Non-Disclosure Agreement**

.net   Online Entity   *Noun*

See Instead: **domain**

net.cop   Online Jargon   *Noun*

Perjorative term referring to a user who's taken upon himself to enforce the unwritten laws of the Internet, such as someone who tries to rally all the participants in a newsgroup to e-mail another user's ISP to complain because he's just been obsessively rude.

net.god   Online Jargon   *Noun*

An individual who's done so much for the Net for so long that everyone everywhere knows him by his first name, like ken, rich, ben, etc.

netiquette   Online Jargon   *Noun*

The rules of polite behavior on Usenet. Rules are many, but most of them come down to "don't pee in the pool." For instance, don't use newsgroups for commercial messages, don't attack people personally or publicly (do it in e-mail), don't crosspost messages to inappropriate newsgroups, and don't encourage flamers.

netizen   Online Jargon   *Noun*

A citizen of the Internet.

Netscape   Online Entity   *Noun*

The Microsoft of the Internet. And when you reflect that Microsoft itself is not the Microsoft of the Internet, well, that should leave you pretty dashed impressed with the power and influence of this company. Also used interchangeably as the name of the company's most influential product, Netscape

Navigator, the most popular (at this writing) web-browser in creation, versions of which exist for Mac, Windows, and every conceivable flavor of UNIX. Netscape has high hopes that it will successfully establish Navigator as the software of choice for these mythical $500 mass-market Internet computers that so many companies are keen to start building.

netstat   Technical Term   *Noun*

UNIX command for testing the validity of an IP address. If you think an address in a message header has been spoofed, for instance, netstat will tell you whether it's valid or not.

netter   Online Jargon   *Noun*

One who uses the Internet. Usually refers exclusively to those whose Internet address does not include the domain compuserve.com, aol.com, msn.com, or any other intergalactic Internet service provider.

NetWare   Product   *Noun*

Novell's omnipresent commercial file-server software.

newbie   Online Jargon   *Noun*

Someone who is new to the online community.

Sometimes, but by no means always, a derogatory term. After all, we were all newbies once.

newsfeed   Technical Term   *Noun*

A service that squirts the whole of Usenet into your computer. An ISP is set up with a newsfeed so it can deliver Usenet newsgroups to its subscribers; end-users certainly wouldn't want to get a newsfeed of their own, unless they're one of those lucky few who've converted a spare bedroom to hold rack after rack of 2-gigabyte drives.

newsgroup   Online Entity   *Noun*

On Usenet, an area for public messages on a defined topic. A newsgroup is the equivalent of a message forum on a commercial service such as CompuServe and America Online (though both also offer access to newsgroups in addition to their own message forums). The naming of newsgroups is vaguely similar to the domain system. In the newsgroup name rec.arts.comics.batman, the periods separate subtopics that narrow the focus of the subject of interest: Recreation/The Arts/Comic Books/Batman. There are thousands of subtopics, but only about a half-dozen worldwide topic groups:

alt—"Alternative" newsgroups, usually unmoderated and usually more freewheeling discussion than found in other topics;

biz—Business;

comp—Computers;

news—Postings and information regarding newsgroups
(such as annoucements of new newsgroups,
information files for specific groups, etc.);

rec—Recreation;

sci—Science;

soc—Society.

There are also topics which are local in scope, such
as "ne," which offers discussion of New England topics,
and "wstd," which I access for news information about
my Internet service provider. Subtopics vary even more
widely. Two useful common subtopics are .answers (as
in "rec.answers") which features FAQ files for each of
that topic's subtopics, and .news, which offers news
and information. Most service providers do not offer
access to the entire list of Usenet newsgroups. Usually
newsgroups are removed to save space and increase
bandwidth on the host computer, but many service
providers remove groups because of their content
matter. If this bugs you, just switch to another provider,
or access *DejaNews'* webpage, which archives and
indexes the entire mess.

.newsrc   Technical Term   *Noun*

The physical file, used by your newsreader program,
that lists all of the Usenet newsgroups available for
reading. *See Also:* **newsgroups**

newsreader   Technical Term   *Noun*

The software you run (either on your desktop PC or on your ISP's hardware) that allows you to read and respond to Usenet postings.

NewsWatcher   Product   *Noun*

John Norstad's freeware newsreader for the Macintosh, of such high quality and so well supported that the rest of the community really hasn't bothered to create a competitor.

Newton   Product   *Noun*

Generic term for any computer that uses Apple's NewtonOS operating system. At this writing, all Newtons are palm-sized slates that accept handwritten text as input. As a happy Newton owner since its introduction, I wish to point out that the writing-recognition feature works, honestly.

NFG   Online Jargon   *Noun*

No Freakin' Good.

NFS   Technical Term   *Noun*

Network File System. A scheme for mounting a net-

worked volume on your local desktop as though it
were physically right there inside your computer.
Quite a bit more convenient than accessing it through
FTP and other transfer protocols.

nine-iron   Online Jargon   *Noun*

Almost at the point where you can say that something
is almost finished. The allusion is to a golfer who's
about to hit a nine-iron shot; this shot should put him
on the green, and from there he's just got a simple
two-putt left.

Example | A nine-iron and then this beta
will be ready to release.

NIS   Technical Term   *Noun*

Network Information Service. Often when you first
configure your Internet software you'll find that you
have to provide the address of your NIS server. This is
the machine on the host that maintains a database listing all of the resources of that host and where they're
found. The NIS server is there so that every single
piece of software doesn't have to record the name of
the host's password file, available services, etc.

nn   Product   *Noun*

New News. More or less the standard newsreader for
those who use shell access to the Internet.

nomex   Online Jargon   *Noun/Adjective*

Fireproof fabric worn by race car drivers. Sometimes used to suggest that you or the original poster is saying something that will attract flamers.

Example
```
<slipping on my Nomex underwear>
Actually, I think Jim Carrey is a
genius, and it's only a matter of
time before he's awarded a special
Nobel Prize for his film oeuvre.
```

Non-Disclosure Agreement

Technical Term   *Noun*

A piece of paper that a computer company forces you to sign when they're about to show you a really hot product months in advance of its release or even its formal announcement. You get this treatment if you're a member of the press, an important software or hardware developer, or maybe just signed up as a pre-release beta tester. Just as cool as getting the chance to see Apple's prototype top-secret combination waffle iron and Internet computer is getting involved in a public online discussion of the project solely because you want to tell the world "Gee, I wish I could reply, but dash it, I'm under nondisclosure on that product."

nonlinear   Online Jargon   *Adjective*

Taking a long and complicated path from start to

finish; sometimes used as a synonym for kluge.

Example | Well, it's a nonlinear solution, but it works.

nontrivial   Online Jargon   *Noun*

Geeky (and popular) way of saying that something is really immensely complicated.

Example | It's really a nontrivial solution, but it works.

notebook   Technical Term   *Noun*

A portable computer that's just heavy and cumbersome enough that you probably wouldn't take it somewhere unless you really thought you'd need it.

NSF   Organization   *Noun*

National Science Foundation. The guys initially responsible for shoveling money from taxpayers' pockets straight into the grand Internet furnace. In recent years, with the ongoing commercialization of the Net, the NSF's monetary contributions are down to minor levels.

NTP   Technical Term   *Noun*

Network Time Protocol. The standard means one computer uses to tell another what time it is.

ob-   Online Style   *Prefix*

Short for "obligatory." In a public message forum (most likely a Usenet newsgroup), the presence of "ob" in front of a word indicates that the poster has begun to feel guilty about letting the message thread drift into hyperspace and wishes to make a good-faith effort to wrestle it back to a topic which is appropriate for this particular forum.

Example

(posted in alt.fan.music.monkees, after talking about Monty Python's "Lumberjack Song" for a mighty long time):

obMonkees: You know, Mike Nesmith wore a hat that, I imagine, is much like something a lumberjack would wear.

ODBC   Technical Term   *Noun*

Open Database Connectivity. A standard (an API, actually) developed by Microsoft for providing database services. That is, an ODBC-compliant database program can easily (well, without soul-sapping difficulty) provide database information to an ODBC-compliant host.

offline   Online Jargon   *Adjective*

(1) Done while not actually connected to another computer; an "offline mailreader" is one that lets you read and compose responses to your electronic mail

while disconnected from your service provider (and therefore without having to pay any connect charges).

(2) Functional, but temporarily not available for use.

(3) Out of the public view, as in meeting someone in a public online conference and wanting to speak with hir privately; "Let's go offline and I'll tell you where to mail that tape."

OLE   Technical Term   *Noun*

Object Linking and Embedding. A Microsoft standard to bring component software features to Windows.

on velvet   Online Jargon   *Adjective*

Sitting pretty, in a good state of affairs.

> **Example** Now, so long as the print server doesn't go down before we have the chance to print the report, we're on velvet.

OnO   Online Jargon   *Noun*

Over and Out. Seen at the end of a one-to-one live chat.

Open Transport   Product   *Noun*

Apple's new fundamental architecture for bringing network services to Macintosh computers. It's a vast improvement over MacTCP because it adds an entire new infrastructure for networking which is infinitely (and, Apple hopes, harmoniously) extensible.

open   Online Jargon   *Adjective*

Describing a hardware or software entity that consists almost entirely of public standards, and does not rely on proprietary, secret technologies. UNIX, for example, is an open operating system, which is why it's been ported to every piece of computing hardware in creation with the exception of certain digital watches. Wintel machines are "open" systems; with the exception of the firmware, almost every component in that box can be ordered individually from any electronics distributor. Macintoshes are "closed" systems; most of the systems that make a Mac work were developed by Apple and are considered trade secrets. This difference accounts for the fact that there are seven times as many Wintel boxes on the planet as there are Macs. The disadvantage of open systems is generally the lack of any one individual or company overseeing the whole mess. This is why adding a hard drive to a Mac consists of plugging in one cable and turning it on, and adding one to a Wintel box can mean endless hours of fixing little problems, each stemming from the fact that the five different companies involved in your open system each had a slightly different idea of what the standard was supposed to be.

OpenDoc   Technical Term   *Noun*

A standard API for component software. An improvement over OLE in that (a) it's an open standard and not proprietary to Windows, (b) it's geared toward creating entire new classes of documents that, technically, were "created" by no one program. Instead of having a word processing document with a spreadsheet table in it, with OpenDoc you just have a blank sheet of paper with text "containers," spreadsheets, graphics, websites, mail, etc., and (c) it will help Apple make a great deal of money. OpenDoc was created by Apple and is supported by just about everyone who doesn't want Microsoft to create and own the standard API for component software. That is, everyone but Microsoft. Rather small-minded behavior, but hey, it's that sort of industry.

OpenLook   Product   *Noun*

Sun's attempt at developing their own GUI. Became pretty popular, but practically died out after everyone jumped on the Motif bandwagon (because Motif is managed and supported by more than just one company, of course). Nonetheless, it's still the standard GUI for Linux.

oracle   Online Entity   *Noun*

(1) A popular corporate database system, but who cares?

(2) More to the point, a netherworldly source of inspiration and information, much like the oracles of old. You may send your requests—illuminations upon life's little worries, solutions to pressing problems of the day,

or or information on the proper use of a drain snake—
to oracle@cs.indiana.edu, and presently you will receive
a complete, if necessarily oracular, answer. Your only
cost is to at some time do a service for the Oracle,
i.e., respond to the supplication of some other poor
slob like yourself. For more info, and sample oracular
readings, visit the rec.humor.oracle newsgroup, or send
e-mail to the oracle with "help" in the subject line.

.org   Online Entity   *Noun*

See *Instead:* **domain**

OSF   Organization   *Noun*

Open Software Foundation. A nonprofit company dedicated to promoting open software. Toward that end,
they've developed versions of UNIX and UNIX GUIs
that can be adapted and used on just about any system.

OTOH   Online Jargon   *Interjection*

On The Other Hand…

-P   Online Style   *Suffix/Modifier*

Adding a "P" to the end of a word turns it into a generalized question. Sending an E-mail with the single
term "ExpoP?" is identical to saying "Hey, a couple of

months ago we discovered that we were both going to MACWORLD Expo and made vague plans to maybe get together for dinner. Are you still going, and do you still want to get some chow? When will you be free?" This results in a spectacular savings of time and bandwidth and good vibes for all.

NB: This convention has its roots in the LISP programming language, and is only understood among the geek set. In an age in which the WWW has brought sophisticated networking services to people who can't even program a VCR, we're always on the lookout for ways to demonstrate that we know more than everyone else.

packet   Technical Term   *Noun*

An easy-to-manage blurb of low-level transmitted data. Rather than squirt something (an E-mail message, a file) from one place to another in one long burst, almost all protocols break the data into packets, which allows more flexibility in how the thing's transmitted.

packet-switching
Technical Term   *Adjective*

Scheme of network data communications by which data is broken up into individual packets, each of which containing information concerning its structure and where it's headed. This allows several different communications to take place simultanously over the same wires and greatly simplifies the installation and management of a network. Packet-switching is a fundamental technology as opposed to a specific, copyrighted scheme.

page   Online Jargon   *Noun*

1) To cause an alert to appear on a specific user's screen, notifying them that you'd like to chat. As this can be more than a little intrusive, you'll not make many friends by tearing them away from their morning mail just to ask them if they're reading their morning mail.

2) Synonym for web page.

page request   Online Jargon   *Noun*

A request of a webserver to see a particular webpage. To see how many people are visiting a page, it's generally more accurate to count these than to count individual hits.

palmtop   Technical Term   *Noun*

A wee li'l computer which, typically, you hold in one hand while you operate it with the other. Most commonly, palmtops are pen-operated devices (like Apple's Newton computers), but many are equipped with truncated keyboards. Most palmtops are designed to be used as personal organizers and data-gathering machines as opposed to things you can word-process on, though there are exceptions.

PANS   Online Jargon   *Noun*

Pretty Amazing New Stuff. Ok, this is just the Internet community getting cute and developing an acronym just to serve as an antonym of POTS. Refers to a somewhat more modern phone service with digital switching and such, offering CallerID, Call Return, ISDN, etc.

parity   Technical Term   *Noun*

An ancient-as-Methuselah method of detecting errors in transmitted data. Basically, the two machines agree beforehand that each byte of data will have either an even number of ones in it, and the transmitting machine will pad each byte as necessary. If the receiving machine receives the number "01011011"—five ones—the receiving machine knows that byte got messed up in transmission. There's also odd parity, and no parity. It's one of the standard communications parameters, but don't sweat it. All of your connections will probably require "no parity," and once you set it, you can forget it.

parse   Technical Term   *Verb*

To read data and make intelligent decisions about what that data means. As a technical terms it refers to operations like parsing an HTML file, in which the browser looks for HTML tags and interprets them to draw the page correctly. Colloquially, refers to the operation of making fundamental sense out of what someone has just told you. "I'm having trouble parsing your meringue recipe; when you say 'You can't beat the egg whites too much' do you mean 'you mustn't over-beat the whites' or 'you can't possibly over-beat the whites, so don't worry about it'?"

patch   Technical Term   *Noun/Verb*

A bit of code added to another piece of software, usually to fix an existing problem with the program. For instance, right after a commercial product is released (DiscoWriter 4.0, say), the fact that now thousands of people are using it instead of dozens of programmers causes several small bugs to finally be discovered. DiscoWare then releases Version 4.01, which has none of the bugs, as well as a patch—a small program which existing users can download that will transmogrify their copies of 4.0 into 4.01. This li'l program is called an updater and can usually be downloaded for free. *See Also:* **bugfix, updater**

path   Technical Term   *Noun*

In the Unix and DOS operating systems, the literal path from the topmost directory of a storage volume all the way to a file, as in "C:\PROGRAMS\WP\ DOCS\NOVELS\THIRD\CHAPTER2.DOC" After an inconvenient number of users imploded after years of dealing with this sort of thing, the industry decided to give graphical user interfaces a go, strictly as a means to stop this erosion of the installed user base.

PBX   Technical Term   *Noun*

Private Branch eXchange. Basically, a local, private phone system, like the system you'd find in a large office. PBXs often present problems for freedom-loving Americans. For one, you often can't just plug a standard modem right into a PBX system; you might need a special adapter. For another, most PBXs don't pass along CallerID information, which means at home your CallerID box will read "(UNAVAILABLE)" instead of "Miserable idiot who's phoned you at dinnertime to try to sell you vinyl siding." Makes you wish we could give Communism a fair try, honestly. I know I do, anyway.

PC Card   Technical Term   *Noun*

A wildly convenient standard for adding hardware devices to a computer, almost exclusively notebook and palmtop computers. All of the electronics for a device are packed onto a circuit board about the size of a business card, which then slides into a PC Card slot without using any tools whatsoever, just like sticking a credit card into an ATM machine. The most common types of PC Card-based devices are modems, Ethernet connectors, and storage devices (like eensy, yet high-capacity, hard drives). Everything is standardized, from the size to the power requirements to the scheme by which the hardware announces its presence to the computer. "Type II" cards are the normal, garden variety standard, but there's also "Type III," twice as thick to accomodate hard drives and other fat devices. In addition to the ease in installing a PC Card, it's also neat in that it's a platform-independent standard. which means you can use your shiny new $250 fax-modem card with your Wintel notebook, your PowerBook, and your Newton.

PCMCIA   Technical Term   *Noun*

Personal Computer Memory Card International Association. "PCMCIA Card" was a term people used before everyone realized that it's really quite a lot to ask of someone to use a seven-syllable technical term before noon; the term was subsequently changed to "PC Card." The acronym is still in currency, as it's the name of the organization which develops and certifies the PC Card standard. *See Also:* **PC Card**

.PCX   Technical Term   *Noun*

File extension for PC Paintbrush graphical file format.

PDA   Technical Term   *Noun*

Personal Digital Assistant. A class of computer that is more powerful than a personal organizer but far smaller and more convenient than a subnotebook computer. Typically, a PDA is focused toward communication and managing personal information, and is a palm-sized unit with a pen interface. When most folks think of a PDA, they think of either the Newton or Sony's MagicLink.

.PDF   Technical Term   *Noun*

See Instead: **Acrobat**

PDP   Technical Term   *Noun*

Personal Digital Processor. Along with the VAX, one of the two venerable old minicomputers made by DEC and sold everywhere. Why, I remember back in high school—this was 1985, mind you—and we had to spend at least a half an hour a day with the school's PDP-11 just keeping it from overheating! And then, when the ADM3As kept fritzing off on us just before Easter vacation, and… *See Also:* **VAX**

perl   Technical Term   *Noun*

Unix's standard scripting language. A popular language for writing CGI's for Unix webservers.

PGP   Technical Term   *Noun*

Pretty Good Privacy. A dashed-near bulletproof public-key encryption system that can provide both authentication and encryption. PGP is freeware and was written at least partly in protest of US government restrictions on the export of decent encryption software.

phreak   Online Jargon   *Noun*

Hacker whose field of interest is the phone system,

especially discovering ways to get free service. Often (and incorrectly) used to refer to a cracker.

pimpware   Online Jargon   *Noun*

Derisive term for a download that is putatively a useful piece of software in its own right, but actually is just part of some huge marketing campaign for a movie or TV show or something. For example, a freeware electronic checkbook program was written to bring simple yet powerful accounting software to those who can't afford commercial software; a pimpware checkbook program has a few basic features, but is designed to get you to look at a picture of Tom Cruise on a regular basis right about when his new movie opens. *See Also:* **public domain software, shareware, demoware, crippleware**

pine   Product   *Noun*

Text-based UNIX program for reading e-mail. Along with elm, the standard for shell accounts.

ping   Technical Term   *Noun*

Packet Internet Groper. A UNIX utility which sends a test packet of data to a specified address and bounces it back. As a result, you can determine whether a certain address is valid or not, how long it takes data to make the trip, how stable the connection is, etc.

pipe   Online Jargon   *Noun*

General term for "the thing which connects your Internet site to the Internet," as in "Well, my company's got a T1 pipe, but we're going to T3 next year." Also a loose synonym for "bandwidth," as in "Dang, this file transfer's taking forever...we've gotta get a bigger pipe."

Pipeline   Online Jargon   *Noun*

The magical imaginary conduit that brings killer technology and features into the desktops of America, e.g. "Well, you can't do that with DiscoWriter 4.0, but I'm told that support of upper and lowercase is in the pipeline for version 4.5..."

Also the name of a large NYC-based ISP.

Pippin   Product   *Noun*

A software and hardware specification for a low-cost (as in $500 or less), CD-ROM based computer, designed by Apple and licensed to other companies. What a Pippin device turns out to be depends on the marketing needs of the licensee: do it one way, and it's a high-end video game machine which can also play Macintosh games. Do it another way, and it's an Internet computer. Do it yet another way, and it's a cable set-top box for interactive television. Pippin might turn out to be a tremendous cash cow for Apple should any of these product categories take off; that's a big "should," however.

pirate   Online Jargon   *Noun/Verb*

To bootleg copyrighted material. Usually refers to software, but also can be applied to any recorded material. Also refers to TV or radio stations that are unlicensed by the FCC and operating illegally.

pizzabox   Online Jargon   *Noun*

A physical desktop computer configuration in which the machine is flat and compact, like a pizza box.

plaintext   Technical Term   *Noun*

Open, unencrypted text. Cryptologists speak of "converting ciphertext to plaintext"—that is, plugging in the password and deciphering the message.

.plan   Technical Term   *Noun*

The file on your UNIX account containing the text that is sent when someone fingers you. Typically contains your name, office hours, your public encryption key, etc.

platform   Technical Term   *Noun*

Generic term referring to the group of computers capable of running a specific family of software.

You've got your Macintosh platform, you've got your Windows platform, etc.

plug-in   Technical Term   *Noun*

A self-contained software component that does nothing on its own but adds a new feature to a specific standalone program when properly installed. Both Netscape and Internet Explorer support the use of plug-ins, which do everything from speak all text on a webpage aloud to allow the user to hot-link data from an Excel spreadsheet.

PMJI   Online Jargon   *Interjection*

Pardon My Jumping In. Used when joining a public message thread that appears to be dominated by just a few people. Netiquette doesn't demand that you use PMJI, but it's considered polite.

Point   Organization   *Noun*

Internet search engine run by Point Communications. Found at http://www.pointcom.com/, Point surveys websites and assigns ratings based on several criteria.

POP   Technical Term   *Noun*

Post Office Protocol. The old protocol for sending and receiving Internet mail. Obsoleted by SMTP.

port address   Technical Term   *Noun*

An address that specifies an Internet application on a machine with a hardwire connection to the Internet. A port address is used when a router, for instance, needs to know where ftp data needs to go; it's sent directly to the app on the machine which handles ftp services for the system.

post, posting   Online Jargon   *Noun, Verb*

A public message. Both can be used as nouns, with posting regarded as a tad more cosmopolitan. As a verb, refers to the act of making anything available to the online community, including a graphic or binary file.

Postmaster   Technical Term   *Noun*

The person at an internet site responsible for that site's mail system. If bhs@lambadaware.com sent you a piece of unsolicited junk mail, you can rat him out by forwarding it to postmaster@lambadaware.com.

POTS   Online Jargon   *Noun*

Plain Old Telephone Service. Good ol' copper wiring that loops to a central office and back. Your basic Mister Magoo phone system with no modern features. *See Also:* **PANS**

pound   Online Jargon   *Noun*

(I) The "#" character.

(2) What you do to people who load up their webpages with frames, flashing text, and animated GIFs.

PPP   Technical Term   *Noun*

Point to Point Protocol. A low-level protocol that allows
sophisticated protocol network connections to take
place over normal telephone lines. Almost always, this
is a TCP connection, but it's a flexible protocol and
can just as readily be used for LocalTalk, for instance.

Private-Key Encryption

Technical Term   *Noun*

General term for a method of encryption in which
there's just one secret password for deciphering the
message. This tends to limit the usefulness of the encryption scheme. *See Also:* **Public-Key Encryption**

Prodigy   Online Entity   *Noun*

Commercial online service that made a splash some
years back by being the first to offer a flat monthly fee
instead of hourly usage rates. This resulted in a titanic
surge of people signing up for the service, most of
whom left upon realizing that the conversations were

awful, there were practically no areas for downloading software, censorship is Stalinesque, and a miserable time was had by all.

propellerhead   Online Jargon   *Noun*

Complimentary term referring to a hacker who's obsessed about technical matters in general. Sometimes used when you admire someone's technical knowledge and skills but aren't sure what shade of beast s/he is, or to refer to someone who knows all about how to use commercial software but nothing about what makes it work. There's a shade of difference between a geek and a propellerhead. A geek has more profound understanding of his or her subject, but the propellerhead has a date for Friday night.

protocol   Technical Term   *Noun*

A communications scheme that folks have developed as a standard; a set of rules governing the format of data exchanged by computers. Different functions require different protocols, which is why we have hyper-text transfer protocol, point-to-point protocol, the gopher protocol, and so forth.

Protocol Stack   Technical Term   *Noun*

See Instead: **stack**

.ps   Technical Term   *Noun*

File extension for PostScript codefile.

Public-Key Encryption

Technical Term   *Noun*

A general term referring to an encryption scheme that involves two passwords. One password is private and is used only to decipher the message; the other is public and is used for encryption (and often is included in a user's online signature or .plan file). This makes the encryption more flexible. It can work as you ordinarily expect a code to work—I use your public key to encrypt my message to you, you use your private key to decipher it—but it also can be used to authenticate a message. You encrypt the message with your super-secret private key and send it to me; if your public key can decipher it, then I can be sure that you and only you could have transmitted it. PGP and RSA are examples of public-key encryption schemes.

public domain software

Technical Term   *Noun*

See Instead: **freeware**

pulse dialing   Technical Term   *Noun*

The sort of dialing noises generated by a rotary telephone. Instead of touch-tones, the phone dials the
number by generating a quaint series of clicks. You
could live and die a hundred lifetimes without ever
having to tell your modem to use pulse dialing.

.qt   Technical Term   *Noun*

File extension for QuickTime movie files.

quick-and-dirty   Online Jargon   *Adjective*

A solution that is a kluge, but then again it was
designed just to get the job done and then be
thrown away.

.ra   Technical Term   *Noun*

File extension for the RealAudio soundfile format.

RBOC   Technical Term   *Noun*

Regional Bell Operating Company. The seven companies that were formed from the break-up of the phone company ("Ma Bell"). Fancy-pants alternative to saying "Baby Bell."

real world   Online Jargon   *Noun*

That which cannot be accessed via a keyboard. A nice place to visit, a good place to swing by when you're out of Coke, but you wouldn't want to live there.

RealAudio   Product   *Noun*

A special format for encoded sound that allows for "live" compression and transmission of digital sound. The most popular sound format for webcasting, as well as the format of choice for long recordings, owing to the superior compression.

reboot   Technical Term   *Noun*

In the technical sense, to shut down a computer and then start it right back up again, in the hopes that whatever problem you're experiencing will go away. It has a similar application colloquially. To start all over again on a project which has far too many problems to even quantify, e.g., "Dr. Martin's made such a mess of the Physics department that the University is going to give it a reboot with Dr. Scholl as the new director" means that Dr. Scholl is expected to rebuild the department from the ground up.

rec.   Online Entity   *Noun*

See Instead: **newsgroup**

reflector site   Technical Term   *Noun*

A site on the Internet which hosts cu-cme content. Usually this means either a video equivalent of an online IRC conference, or a "special event" Internet broadcast, like some pitiful Dayton garage band's "worldwide live debut" of their new hit single.

relative URL   Technical Term   *Noun*

A URL that specifies a link to a file, but does not provide the precise path to the file. Useful in that it will allow a browser to locate "logo.jpg" even if you change the name of the folder it's in, but nonetheless a scheme which gives software limitless opportunities to screw things up. *See also:* **URL**

remailer   Technical Term   *Noun*

An online entity that takes an incoming message, strips all of its source information, and then sends it on to its destination or another remailer. Remailers are used to send mail anonymously. *See Also:* **cloak, morphing**

Retcon   Online Jargon   *Verb*

In an ongoing episodic storyline (like a comic book, a series of movie sequels, a TV series), the act of rewriting a part of the storyline that has suddenly become inconvenient. Say a soap star suddenly demands twice as much money and the producers get so mad that they write an episode in which his character is shoved into an active volcano and actually seen burning to death. If two years later the star's movie career hasn't worked out and the producers hire him back on at half his original salary, they'll have to retcon his death scene by saying that, actually, he had managed to cling to the rim where he was rescued by a secret order of monks.

RFC   Technical Term   *Noun*

Request For Comment. Specifically refers to a formal open call for people to take a look at a new proposed Internet standard and tell the standards body that they've got their collective heads lodged in a major collective body cavity. However, the term's been proletariatized to refer to any announcement that asks the general public for its opinions on something.

RJ11   Technical Term   *Noun*

The technical name for the modular connector used in phone jacks, among other things.

RLE   Technical Term   *Noun*

Run Length Encoding. Next to LZW, the most pervasive fundamental data-compression algorithm.

rockwell chipset   Technical Term   *Noun*

Modem firmware designed and manufactured by
Rockwell. In the distant past when faxmodems were a
novelty, "features the Rockwell chipset" was generally
used as a synonym for "has fax features." Today, almost
every modem has chips made by Rockwell, so it's sort
of a useless term.

rollover   Online Jargon   *Noun/Verb*

Every message base (commercial message forums,
Usenet newsgroups, etc.) can hold only so many messages. When it reaches capacity, new messages are left
as old messages are deleted or expire. This is known
as rollover and is sometimes used to gauge the popularity of a message area.

Example Messages in the SHOWBIZ forum usually rollover in about five days.

root   Technical Term   *Noun*

In UNIX, the name of the account owned by the system administrator. If you have root access, basically

you're "God of the Pond" and the users therein live and die at your pleasure. As you might guess, the goal of system crackers is to acquire root access.

ROTFL   Online Jargon   *Noun*

Rolling On The Floor Laughing. A reaction to something funny someone's posted. Once you've mastered Internet communications, you may opt to roll your own flavors of this term. You might come across an acronym like ROTFLOTDADTSAITPOAOB. The idea is that you'll be curious enough to ask the sender what it means, and he can proudly reply "Rolling On The Floor Laughing, Out The Door And Down The Street And Into The Path Of An Oncoming Bus." Now, are you sure you want to join this here Internet community? *See Also:* **grin, emoticons**

router   Technical Term   *Noun*

(1) A machine on the Internet that does nothing but examine every packet of data that passes through it and directs it toward its target.

(2) That which "New Yankee Workshop" TV host Norm Abram can build absolutely anything with. I'm sorry, I know this is off the subject, but I watch this show every week and I honestly think the man deserves credit. Give the man a router, a biscuit-joiner, and a pile of scrap lumber and he can build you a

power yacht…and that's including the motor and the
crew. Honestly, my hat's off.

RS-232   Technical Term   *Noun*

....

Recommended Standard 232. The ubiquitous standard
for serial communications, used everywhere. Every single modem connects to your computer via RS-232,
but nonetheless, you know, it's just a recommendation.
Do keep in mind that you always have the option of
just reading a book instead.

RSA   Technical Term   *Noun*

....

Rivest, Shamir, Adleman. A public-key encryption system that provides both encryption and authentication.
RSA is a patented system that RSA Data Security
licenses out to many software companies.

RSI   Technical Term   *Noun*

....

Repetitive Stress Injury. The sort of cumulative injuries
you suffer as the result of performing the same move-
ments over and over again, like when you bang on
your notebook for ten hours a day. Hackers fear RSIs
the same way that people in discos during the
Seventies feared STDs (sexually transmitted
diseases). RSIs are serious, serious business and can
lead to permanent impairment and pain. Search for

any of the dozens of good online guides to avoiding RSIs, and until you do, maintain good posture and take breaks from your keyboard every fifteen minutes or so.

RSN   Online Jargon   *Noun*

Real Soon Now. Sometimes actually means Real Soon Now. Usually, though, it's used sarcastically, meaning it'll happen, but only God knows when, as in "DiscoWriter 5.0 is due to be released RSN."

.rtf   Technical Term   *Noun*

File extension for Rich Text Format. Microsoft's early attempt at an independent file format that would allow a formatted document written with one word processor to be imported into a different word processor with its formatting intact.

RTFAQ   Online Jargon   *Noun*

Read the FAQ.

RTFM   Online Jargon   *Noun*

(1) Read The Freakin' Manual. You probably knew that already if you've ever called for technical support, but the other definition of the term is—

(2) the name of the FTP site that archives each and every one of the legion of FAQ files posted on Usenet newsgroups. If you're interested in learning the basics of a subject, or want to find Internet resources related to a subject, your first place to go is ftp://rtfm.mit.edu/pub/usenet-by-group/ (or its mirror site, http://www.cis.ohio-state.edu/hypertext/faq/usenet/FAQ-List.html)/

run-time version   Technical Term   *Noun*

Oftentimes, a file you download requires a commercial product in order to make it run on your machine; for instance, a BASIC program that needs the BASIC programming environment it was created in. For good will and, not the least, to get the public at large to depend on their products, a company might create a special free "run-time version" of their commercial product, one which has no real features of its own but allows the product's files to run.

s/n ratio   Online Jargon   *Noun*

See *Instead:* **signal-to-noise ratio**

scalable   Online Jargon   *Noun*

You've got these people, see, who are nice, decent folk but not very technically oriented. But they see all of those mighty geeks over there, romping and gamboling online and at industry conferences, swapping acronyms and jargon with great abandon, and you know, they feel sort of left out. So, they develop dopey "insider" terms of their own, like "scalable." You want to know what "scalable" means? It means "upgradable." Nope, it doesn't add an extra nuance or emphasis anywhere. It's just there so that dopey middle-managers can point to the purchase order and tell their bosses, "And, this system is completely scalable within the existing architecture!" instead of "If I loused up and didn't order enough memory for everyone, we can just buy more and install it." The geeks have tried to rehabilitate this term by using it to refer to a machine that has been designed so that you can add processing power without replacing the whole box (by replac-ing the existing processor with a more powerful one, or adding multiple processors). Salt of the earth, those computer geeks.

sci.   Online Entity   *Noun*

See *Instead:* **newsgroup**

scratch   Technical Term   *Noun*

Something that has been created for temporary use; hence, Netscape's "Scratch Files" are files the program creates on your hard drive to keep some information handy, but are deleted after they're used.

screen name   Online Jargon   *Noun*

The name you go by on a certain online service. A

screen name may or may not be your actual name;
often, users choose an alternative nickname (RedSox_
Faithful, NothingLike_RichardGere) just for fun or to
protect their privacy. Some services encourage the
use of screen names, to the extent of allowing one
account to have a half-dozen screen names defined
for it. *See Also:* **handle**

scripting   Technical Term   *Noun*

The control or automation of an application through a
pre-prepared list of English-like commands. A "scripting
language" can be every bit as powerful as a mainstream
programming language like C, but is given this second-
class status because such programs can't run unless
another piece of software is interpreting it, line for
line. Perl is the standard scripting language for UNIX.

sdk   Technical Term   *Noun*

Software Developer's Kit. A set of software and
libraries that allows a programmer to develop software that supports (or enhances) someone else's
software. *See Also:* **api**

search engine   Technical Term   *Noun*

Any software entity that provides search services. But
as a practical matter, almost always refers to a public
Internet resource that allows you to search the whole

of the Internet—usually folks are interested in finding websites, but FTP sites and Usenet newsgroups can also be searched—for key words and phrases you specify. The popular engines can be broken down into three vague groups. First, there are the "Yellow Pages" type of engines, whose contents are weeded out and organized by humans. The chief advantage is that it's easy to find something interesting when you're not certain exactly what you're looking for; for example, if you're wondering where you can get a current weather forecast, you can find it with just three or four mouse clicks. Second, the "Siskel & Ebert" type, which are similar to the Yellow Pages but also offer objective reviews of each site in the database. Third, you've got the ones that value quantity over quality. "Spider" programs explore the Net all on their own, reporting back to their overlords on all of the webpages they've discovered. They're not as easy to use as the others (you need to have a specific idea of what you're looking for) but they're exhaustive; they're also good in that they're the best way to find "an article about Richard Feynman's theories of quantum electrodynamics" as opposed to "physics sources." URLs for specific search engines are listed under their individual entries. For "Yellow Pages," check out Yahoo (IMHO the best starting point for new users of the Web), Lycos, and Infoseek. For website reviews, check out Point and Magellan. For exhaustive web searching, check out AltaVista. And for searching months and months of archived Usenet postings, try DejaNews.

self-extracting archive

Technical Term   *Noun*

....

See Instead: **archiver**

September Slug   Online Jargon   *Noun*

A pernicious and predictable flavor of newbie. The darkest hour of the Internet, the span of time that causes the old hands to just switch to CompuServe for the duration or to just unplug all their computers for good measure, is September. This is when incoming college freshmen first get their university Internet access, which leads, of course, to endless newism, usually in the form of pig-headed cloth-eared ignorance. September 1 is a good time to hit the alt.fan.letterman newsgroup and read messages from different new users reading "LETTERMAN SUCKS!!! LENO RULEZ!!! — CAPTAIN CYBERDOMINION" Fortunately, by October, these debbies have either wised up, had their Internet access pulled, or flunked out.

server   Technical Term   *Noun*

A machine on a network that serves other machines on the network. Well, you see the problem here. It's a very basic term that means so little when it's out of context, and in the end it's sort of self-explanatory. A webserver is therefore a computer that sits around all day waiting for another computer to ask it to send over some webpages. A mailserver is a machine that processes all of the mail for the network. When someone on the network sends mail, it's first sent to the server, which then sends it to its destination (or to another mailserver closer thereto). A faxserver does nothing but receive documents from other computers all day and then spits them out as a fax to whatever phone number it's told to.

set-top box   Technical Term   *Noun*

A hole on the top of your television set in which enormous communications companies keep throwing money. It's the mythical cable box that also allows access to the Internet, either allowing the delivery of normal Internet services (mail, the Web) or a special subset (like movies-on-demand and interactive television). At this writing, the only thing it's delivered is hundreds of press releases from dozens of corporations that wish to announce that their nonexistent set-top box is much, much better than anyone else's nonexistent set-top box.

Setext   Technical Term   *Noun*

A format for tagging a text document to indicate its content's structure. A popular scheme for e-zines and other electronic newsletters, before the Web hit it big.

SGML   Technical Term   *Noun*

A sort of rudimentary page-description language. It's a set of published standards for describing the format, structure, and content of a document. In practical terms, it describes a family of page-markup languages. If you had never heard of HTML but you were told that it was an SGML markup language, your reaction would be "Oh, Lord, I'm going to be surrounding words with <blah> and </blah> all summer, aren't I?"

shareware   Technical Term   *Noun*

"Try before you buy" software. You may download the complete, finished version of the software (or get a copy from a friend). If you find yourself getting solid use out of the thing, you're honor-bound to send the author the reasonable registration fee requested. Downloading shareware and using it for years without sending in the shareware fee is the world's seventh leading cause of bad karma, a fact which is of particular interest to people who spend any amount of time on our nation's highways.

shell account, shell access

Technical Term   *Noun*

An account with your ISP that allows you to bring up a UNIX prompt on the ISP's host computer. The advantage of shell access is that it allows you to use a whole boatload of sophisticated UNIX tools for accessing and managing the Internet; the disadvantage is that 99.44% of all the cool Internet software requires a TCP connection to the Internet. Savvy folks thumb their noses at this limitation, however: by installing the right software on your UNIX host (tia or the freeware slirp), your shell account can behave just like a PPP connection.

shockwave   Technical Term   *Noun*

A plug-in for web-browsers that allows them to play animations created with Macromedia Director, a commercial program for developing multimedia animation.

SHTTP   Technical Term   *Noun*

Secure Hypertext Transfer Protocol. RSA-based encryption scheme that allows secure interaction with a website. If you're searching on the Web and finally find a company that can sell you that Theremin you've always wanted, you really shouldn't just transmit your Mastercard number unprotected. Commercial sites will use an encrypted standard like SHTTP so that if the data is intercepted before it reaches its destination (remember, your credit card number can bop through a dozen systems before it reaches the server at Theremin City), it'll come through as unreadable garbage.

.sig   Technical Term   *Noun*

The ASCII "signature" at the bottom of a message, composed by the sender and automatically appended by the sender's mail or news program. Usually the .sig contains items like the sender's full name, what they do for a living, the URL for his or her website, and a quote or slogan. *NB:* A little restraint is called for when choosing a .sig. A half a dozen lines is about the maximum length and, in fact, many news and mail programs impose a limit of four. *See Also:* **sigfile**

Example	
	``` ============================== Dr. Gern Blanstev, Ph.D http://www.usndh.edu/blanstev/ University of Southern North Dakota At Hoople "Power is the only drug regulated by the SEC instead of the FDA." ```

sigfile   Technical Term   *Noun*

The file containing your online signature, or .sig. See Also: .sig

signal-to-noise ratio

Online Jargon   *Noun*

Term used to describe the amount of useful or entertaining stuff found on an online entity as compared to the amount of garbage. A David Letterman newsgroup that features intelligent discussion, news about past and future shows, and participation by actual writers and producers has a high signal-to-noise ratio (or is "high bandwidth"). A Letterman newsgroup in which most of the postings are pointless discussions of the best Stupid Pet Trick and conjectures about the sexual orientations of the band has a low signal-to-noise ratio (or is "low bandwidth"). Also called s/n ratio.

.SIT   Technical Term   *Noun*

File extension for Stuffit archive file format.

slash   Online Jargon   *Noun*

(1) The "/" character.

(2) What is done to people who load up their webpages with frames, flashing text, and animated GIFs after they've been pounded.

SLIP   Technical Term   *Noun*

Serial Line Internet Protocol. Like PPP, a scheme for establishing a net connection over a phone line. Practically obsolete, though, because it's slower, less reliable, and less flexible than PPP.

slirp   Product   *Noun*

A freeware offering for UNIX systems that lets users of dial-up accounts access the system as though they had PPP accounts. *See Also:* **TIA**

smilies   Online Style   *Interjection*

See Instead: **emoticons**

SMTP   Technical Term   *Noun*

Simple Mail Transfer Protocol. The protocol used to store, send, and retrieve mail via TCP.

smurf, smurfette   Online Jargon   *Noun*

Someone who posts regularly on a newsgroup or forum but rarely adds anything substantive to the conversation. Usually it's something cute and fluffy posted chiefly to remind everyone that the smurf is part of the gang.

snail mail   Online Jargon   *Noun*

Analog e-mail. The sort that is inscribed on mashed pulp substrate, encapsulated in a semi-secure archive of similar substrate with added mammal extract to ensure the archive's integrity, and delivered to the addressee using a quaint procedure involving kindly men and women dressed in sharp blue uniforms.

.snd   Technical Term   *Noun*

File extension for Apple "Sound" file format.

<snip>   Online Jargon   *Noun*

In a reply to a message, indicates that some of the original message's text has been deleted here.

SO   Online Jargon   *Noun*

Significant Other. These kids today, with their computers and their Internet and whatnot are too serious to call their girlfriends and boyfriends by their IEEE-sanctioned names and, Lord knows, they don't believe in marriage, so they refer to their Main Squeezes as

SO's. My SO, I am proud to point out, is the lovely and talented Heather B.

soc.　Online Entity　*Noun*

See *Instead:* **newsgroup**

social engineering
Online Jargon　*Noun*

Hacking wetware, or finding a solution to a problem by interacting with people and not hardware. For instance, if you needed an account on a company's computer system but didn't actually work there, you could hack the password file, exploit holes in the firewalls to become superuser, create a secret and blind account for yourself, et cetera. Or, you could just call the system administrator, claim to be a new hire, and convince him to establish a new account for you. That's social engineering. Significantly less messy, plus it helps you work on those all-important interpersonal skills.

socket　Technical Term　*Noun*

An electronic address that specifies an individual IP address and an application running therein.

sockets　Technical Term　*Noun*

An API specifically for adding TCP functions to a program.

spam   Online Jargon   *Noun*

··

This calls for a little story. Imagine a scene set in
Boston's Museum of Fine Arts. A large crowd of people is around Copley's famous portrait of Paul Revere,
as there always is. In the front of the crowd is the
owner of a used-tire store. "Wow!" he thinks, looking
around. "A thousand people an hour must come
through and look at this!" And without further ado, he
pulls out a can of spray paint and writes "GET YOUR
WHEEL DEALS AT PAT HEPKE'S USED TIRE
RODEO" in purple across the Copley and the wall it's
hanging on. "I have a perfect right to put my ad here!"
he shouts, as a gaggle of elderly museum guards wrestle him to the ground. "This is a public museum
owned by the public!!!" And thus you understand
Spamming. Spamming is the all–too–common practice
of some shyster outfit using a special mail program to
post their advertisements (usually for phone-sex lines,
bankruptcy, credit and immigration attorneys, and
other upstanding organizations) on every single public
Usenet newsgroup everywhere, regardless of topic.
The effect is like tossing a can of Spam into the
whirling blades of a ceiling fan—useless and bother-
some crud is splattered all over the joint without
rhyme or reason. The word is taken from a Monty
Python routine where a pleasant, if banal, conversation
is overwhelmed with loudly shouted choruses of
"Spam, spam, spam, spam...." Often also applied to any
example of unsolicited junk e-mail or any inappropriate crossposting. As with the classic Spammer, an
expletive-ridden threat of litigation and severe bodily
harm is usually the way to respond.

spider   Technical Term   *Noun*

Software that explores the World Wide Web on its own, returning indexes of the webpages it finds. This information is then put into a master database that search engines use to find webpages of a specified subject.

splat   Online Jargon   *Noun*

The asterisk ("*"). And do me a favor: don't pronounce it "Aster-ick." Oh, sure, it didn't bother me at first, but then week after week I heard more and more people mispronouncing it, and, you know, every time I hear it I get pushed just one electron-width closer to the point where I'm forced to get an axe and…well, look, just don't mispronounce it, OK?

Also sometimes refers to the symbol on Apple's "Command" key.

spoiler   Online Jargon   *Noun*

In a public or private message about a movie (or a book or any other suspenseful creation), the word SPOILER in either the subject or the body of the message indicates that the message contains info that would spoil the ending for people who haven't yet seen the film. An almost mandatory practice of online etiquette. The Spoiler Warning is so widely used that many newsreaders can detect a special "spoiler" character (control-l) which causes it to scroll down an entire screen before displaying the next line.

Example	It really was a surprise. It's sort of like when I was a kid and SPOILER WARNING: STAR WARS SAGA found out that Luke Skywalker's dad was Darth Vader!

spoofed   Online Jargon   *Adjective*

General term referring to a piece of mail whose origin is suspect.

SQL   Technical Term   *Noun*

Structured Query Language. A standardized quasi-English simple language for retrieving data from a compliant database.

S-registers   Technical Term   *Noun*

A bank of your modem's memory that stores a pile of variables concerning the modem's operations, such as how many rings to wait before answering the phone, what protocols to specifically use or not use, what sort of phone line to expect, etc. Each S-register is associated with a specific feature or operation, and these operations are modified by stashing a specific number in a specific register. For instance, the AT command ATS0=2 puts the number 2 into register 0, which means "automatically answer the phone after two rings."

SSL   Technical Term   *Noun*

....

Secure Sockets Layer. RSA-based encryption scheme
proposed by Netscape for protecting the whole of
WWW data communications. Make no mistakes,
Netscape is all hot and itchy about the prospect of
interstate banking on the Web, and realizes that until
there's a bulletproof way to transmit transactions over
the Net, it just ain't gonna happen.

stack   Technical Term   *Noun*

....

In networking, refers to the multi-layered hierarchical
arrangement of protocols that data percolates
through as it makes its way through your computer.
For instance, in the OSI standard, the bottom-most
level in the stack is the program you're actually interacting with (such as your mailreader program); the
very top is the physical wire running out of your computer and into the network, and there are five layers
in between. Suffice to say that when someone refers
to a "stack" as regards communications, he's referring
to the bundle of protocols that lets you interact with
a network. If someone comes up to you and says
"Hey, did you hear that Casio's about to release a
databank watch with a TCP stack built-in?" He's all
excited because he'll be able to get his Internet mail
from his wristwatch. Which, frankly, is a pretty damned
interesting project. I know I'd buy one.

stale link   Online Jargon   *Noun*

....

On a webpage, a link to a page that no longer exists.

Usually a link goes stale because the page has shut down or moved. *See Also:* **link**

Star-Dot-Star   Online Jargon   *Noun/Verb*

See Instead: ***.***

starting point   Online Jargon   *Noun*

A "cover page" for the Internet. Egalitarian Internet Service Providers set up their software so that when new users fire it up for the first time, the web-browser will take them immediately to the service's "Starting Point" page, containing a bunch of popular links to get folks started right away. Probably the most popular starting point is Yahoo.

studlytext   Online Jargon   *Noun*

Undulating waves of capitalization in text, such as ThIS IS HarD To rEaD, iSn'T iT? *See Also:* **leeguage**

Stuffit   Product   *Noun*

The name of the de facto standard format for archived files on the Macintosh, as well as the commercial program which creates them. Stuffit is available in both commercial and shareware/freeware versions.

Stupid, Stupid Rat Creatures!

Online Jargon   *Noun*

Exclamation of disapproval. From the wunnerful comic book "Bone." Often customized to suit the occasion, most often along the lines of "Stupid, stupid end-users! Mac'sbug must load before all other system extensions!"

subgroup   Online Entity   *Noun*

A newsgroup one or more levels down in the Usenet hierarchy, for discussion of a related subtopic. alt.fan.clint-howard.movies would be a subgroup of alt.fan.clint-howard. Created when the "parent" news-group becomes so popular that the number of post-ings far outstrips anyone's ability to keep up.

subnotebook   Technical Term   *Noun*

A portable computer one step smaller than a Notebook. Typically, subs are significantly slimmer and lighter than a notebook, but still have a full-sized key-board and a display with the same pixel dimensions as its larger brethren. A subnotebook usually trades off significant creature comforts, though, like a disk drive, PC Card expandability, color, and the like.

superuser   Technical Term   *Noun*

On a system, the account(s) that grant absolute,

unlimited, dare I say Zarathusian powers to its owners. You know, creating and deleting user accounts, granting users extra powers or removing powers at their sole discretion, deciding which software gets loaded onto the system and who gets to use it, etc. Send them brownies. Do not question them. They are blameless, holy creatures, just like cows.

sysadmin   Technical Term   *Noun*

System Administrator. Synonym for Sysop, though the term implies more power.

sysop   Technical Term   *Noun*

System Operator. One of the people who run an online entity, though not necessarily the superuser. A sysop's powers depend on what sort of entity s/he's the sysop of—a Compuserve sysop just moderates one of the online forums, an ISP's sysop might be in charge of making sure the tape back-ups run OK, and a BBS sysop runs the entire show.

system   Technical Term   *Noun*

(1) (cap.) The specific term for Macintosh operating system files, as in "I'm running System 7.1, but when I buy that new machine, I'll definitely switch to System 7.5.3"

(2) When used as an adjective, "system software" or "system-level software" refers to software that is required by the operating system and the hardware, as opposed to software which is used by the end-user. A printer driver is an example of system-level software.

T1   Technical Term   *Noun*

OK, well, here I'm in a quandary. This is a Random House Dictionary, after all, so I'm obligated to say that T1 is a direct point-to-point cabling specification for high-speed digital communications over copper wire, supporting 24 channels of 64Kbps communications each. But sitting right here, even though I'm about seven months in the past and thousands of miles away, I can just hear the hairs on the back of your neck raising in confusion. That is why I am, instead, going to give you the practical and simple definition: a hard connection to the Internet that gives you wicked fast access. There. I think I'm doing the right thing here.

T3   Technical Term   *Noun*

The same sort of general idea as a T1 circuit, only fiber-optic and 44.74 Mbps. That is, wicked wicked wicked wicked wicked wicked "Whoah, Nelly, why don't I just download the whole Library of Congress during my lunch break," fast.

tag   Technical Term   *Noun*

In an HTML document (like the source code for a

webpage), a command enclosed by angle brackets (<>) that tells the browser how that item should be handled. For instance, <i>this statement is enclosed by beginning and ending italics tags</i>.

talk, ntalk   Technical Term   *Noun*

Standard UNIX programs for one-to-one live chat. Broadly, any program or protocol for live chat over a network.

TAPI   Technical Term   *Noun*

Telephony Application Programming Interface. An API and physical specification for allowing computers to act like telephones.

tar   Product   *Noun*

A UNIX utility for compressing files. Files compressed with tar, amazingly enough, have the extention .tar after them.

Tarim   Online Jargon   *Noun*

In the *Cerebus* comic book, the name of God. Used similarly online, particularly if one somewhat mockingly doesn't want to offend the sort of people who get offended by people who say, "For God's sake, man!"

TCP/IP Technical Term *Noun*

The fundamental protocol which connects all the hardware of the Internet together. It's supported by every operating system on every platform (well, all the ones that matter, anyway) and as such it's what makes the Internet happen. It stands for "Transmission Control Protocol/Internet Protocol." Colloquially, it can be used to mean "this product can work over a network/the Internet," as in "We're proud to announce the first solitaire game that supports TCP/IP."

Telnet Product *Noun*

Standard UNIX protocol and program for connecting to a remote host from the host you're logged into now. As a verb, to use Telnet or connect to (a site) using Telnet. Originally, Telnet was your only tool for surfing the Net; these days, most netizens live full and happy lives without even knowing of its existence. Still, it's a useful piece of software to know. For instance, if you're on the road and 3000 miles away from your hometown ISP, you can place a local call into a nearby ISP and Telnet home from there, using an online mail-reader like elm to keep on top of your mailbox.

10BASE-T Technical Term *Noun*

A popular standard for cabling an Ethernet network.

thrashed   Online Jargon   *Verb/Adjective*

A more intense version of hosed—damaged, spectacularly and (usually) beyond repair. Usually refers to physical damage as opposed to logical damage, and often refers to damage which you witnessed but were powerless to stop. *See Also:* **hosed, throcked**

Example | DAMN!!! The airline baggage system thrashed my server equipment!!!

thread   Online Jargon   *Noun*

A series of public messages and the responses to those messages that, when read in sequence, comprise a single "conversation." Theoretically, all of the messages in a thread center around the same subject, but then again in theory, it's possible to make a million bucks in real estate with just $100 down. Get real. What usually happens is topic drift. Most online entities maintain threads automatically—reading one message allows you to naturally read all of its replies, and all of the replies to the replies, etc. Some, most prominently AOL, make following a thread more difficult. *See Also:* **topic drift**

throcked   Online Jargon   *Noun/Adjective*

A synonym for thrashed, used when you've gotten over the initial shock and have accepted it as merely the cost of doing business in a Universe which was slapped together in six days by a guy who left town

without a trace immediately thereafter. *See Also:*
hosed, thrashed

throughput   Technical Term   *Noun*

Simple definition: the effective speed of something as
opposed to the actual speed. Practical definition: A
special code-word people use to describe the speed
of something, which indicates that somehow, somewhere, there's some sort of monkey business going on
with the math. For instance, an ad for a v.34 modem
might boast "Throughput of up to 57.6 kbps!" In reality, a v.34 modem can't pump data through a phone
line any faster than 28.8, but under optimal conditions
the modem's built-in data compression can squeeze
the data down 50% during transmission. Ergo, the
modem is communicating at 28.8 but it's achieving the
results of 57.6 transmission.

TIA   Online Jargon   *Interjection*

Thanks In Advance

tia   Product   *Noun/Adjective*

The Internet Adapter. A piece of commercial software
that runs on your ISP's UNIX system allowing a normal dialup line to act like a sophisticated PPP connection. This means that instead of being limited to text-
based UNIX Internet tools, you have the whole rain-

bow of TCP web-browsers, mailreaders, newsreaders, etc. to choose from. At least you could before "slirp" was released, which does everything tia did and was free. Free is a difficult price point to comprehend, and so tia is no more.

tilde   Online Jargon   *Noun/Adjective*

The "~" character. In jargon, translates to "about or around."

Example | The MST3K movie premiere is at 9; what say we meet in front of the theater ~8?

tin   Product   *Noun*

A character-based newsreader for UNIX systems.

TLA   Online Jargon   *Noun*

Three Letter Acronym. Yes, after so many years of keeping thousands of acronyms straight, you start to get just a bit potty about the things.

TNX   Online Jargon   *Interjection*

Thanks

tool   Online Jargon   *Verb*

To work very, very hard, particularly when its clear to you that the person who's making you work like this values the appearance of work more than they do the result.

topic drift   Online Jargon   *Noun*

The inevitable situation that develops when a message thread has gone on for dozens of replies and the "Subject" line no longer bears any relevance to what's being discussed.

tower   Online Jargon   *Noun*

A physical computer design that looks like an upright narrow coffee table.

trash   Online Jargon   *Verb*

To destroy.

trivial   Online Jargon   *Adjective*

So simple to understand that there's really no need to explain it here.

    Actually, I've just read that definition back and it's

occurred to me that you might have gotten the impression that I was being condescending. Believe me, I'm fully aware that you bought this book because there are plenty of terms out there you might not be familiar with, and as such I would be ignoring my mandate if I claimed that a certain term was beneath me to even define.

Furthermore, I mean, what kind of a jerk goes out of his way to put the term in a dictionary and then haughtily not even define it? So please, I just want to be extra certain that you understand that the first paragraph here is just literally the definition of the term. I mean, ask anyone: I'm a jovial, salt-of-the-earth type who gets on rather well with people. Very approachable, friendly, always there to patiently explain things when asked. So let's just move along and say no more about this.

Trojan Horse   Technical Term   *Noun*

A nasty piece of software masquerading as a benign piece of software; e.g., any program with the Microsoft logo on it. No, no, that's not fair at all. A real trojan horse would be a game which is designed to erase your hard drive after five minutes of play, for instance. Does the sporting thing and shows its true colors straightaway, unlike Windows, which strings you along for months, when all the while you're blaming yourself for everything that goes wrong. So when you get down to it, Windows is more like a spouse.

NB: sometimes applied to a program that has been infected with a virus; this is an incorrect, overly broad usage.

trolling   Online Jargon   *Noun*

Crafting and posting a message (a "troll") specifically intended to attract the hyperbolic and unfocused rage of a flamer. A troll typically expresses a simple and basic question in a particularly long-winded and clueless fashion, or expresses sentiments that will likely provoke an enraged response (e.g. posting "Why don't you guys realize that you're trying to undermine our family values?" to soc.motss, a gay newsgroup). An explanation of what makes reading the responses to your troll amusing is beyond the scope of this reference book and the reader is instead to consult Douglas Adams' *Dirk Gently's Molistic Detective Agency*. It has no illumination to offer on the subject, but is a good read and a far more pleasureable way to spend the afternoon than attempting to understand the thought processes of the sort of people whose entire lives revolve around flaming, trolling, and their *Baywatch* tapes.

Trumpet Winsock   Product   *Noun*

A shareware software package that allows users of Windows 3.x to use TCP/IP programs. The de facto standard.

TTFN   Online Jargon   *Interjection*

Ta Ta For Now.

turner's law   Online Jargon   *Noun*

"The feature set of any piece of software will expand

until it is able to read mail. Those that do not will be driven out of business by those which do." Originally just a funny saying, but man, I just got a press release for a spreadsheet program that really can fetch your Internet mail!

TWAIN   Technical Term   *Noun*

Toolkit Without An Interesting Name. A standardized software interface for grabbing an image from the Real World (through a scanner, a video camera, etc) and throwing it into the computer. TWAIN was developed as an alternative to the makers of an image-editing program having to specifically write code to support every such device under the sun; now, all you need is the TWAIN driver for the device and you're golden. And doesn't the acronym provide an illustration of some quandary of mathematical set theory or something? Just think about it, you know? Should we allow this sort of thing to go on?

tweak   Online Jargon   *Noun/Verb*

A small modification done to try to fix or improve something. Usually refers to things like increasing your disk cache by 5K every day until you find the perfect value, but also can refer to a general enhancement, as in "Hey, there's a tweak for System 7.5.3 that turns the trash can into a paper shredder, complete with sound effects!" Also used as a verb.

.txt   Technical Term   *Noun*

File extension for an ordinary text file.

UART   Technical Term   *Noun*

Universal Asynchronous Receiver Transmitter. Generalized term for the IC in a Wintel box that is responsible for the serial input and output of a computer. Famous in the Wintel world for the immensely frustrating error message "Looking for UART at <address>," which means that the easiest solution to the problem is to buy another computer or try to find another line of work that doesn't require you to have a modem connected to your machine. Now, a Mac owner probably never even heard of a UART in his life. But then, you're probably sick of hearing stuff like that by now…

Unicode   Technical Term   *Noun*

A humongous extension to the ASCII standard designed to provide a standard code for every conceivable character in every conceivable language, including a pictograph of that nutty "Keep on Truckin'!" guy. He cracks me up every time.

Uniform Resource Locator
Technical Term   *Noun*

See *Instead:* **URL**

UNIX   Product   *Noun*

Uniplexed Information and Computing System. The

third most popular religion (right behind Christianity)
and the fifth most popular basis upon which to start a
fistfight (behind vague allegations about one's mother's
proclivity for swimming after troop ships). UNIX is an
operating system that earns fanatical devotion among
its users and is the absolute backbone of the Internet.
UNIX is an overwhelming force of nature because: 1)
It's an open system. That is, UNIX isn't so much a specific operating system as it is a set of specifications for
an operating system; therefore, there are dozens of
different flavors of UNIX that can run on literally any
machine worth mentioning. All of UNIX's secrets are
out, which means that any programmer can enhance
or extend the OS in any manner he or she sees fit.
2) It's an open system. That is, it was designed with a
core purpose of allowing machines to link up and
share information. Intimate networking is one of the
ground-floor features of UNIX, not an exotic add-on.
3) It's powerful. The architecture of the OS and the
variety of its tools are so deep and broad you get the
impression that if there's ever a need to calculate the
exact time, date and place of the Second Coming and
furthermore to guess the Messiah's weight to within
three grams, there's probably already a UNIX shell
script somewhere that can figure out the answer in
about eleven minutes. 4) It's the most heavily evange-
lized OS on the planet. People who use it, love it, and
they want you to love it, too. Towards that end, most
of the best and most important software is free, written for the good of the UNIX community. It is because of these strengths that even non-UNIX users
reap the benefits of the Internet. None of this would
have been possible without the work of hundreds of
thousands of UNIX programmers creating new and
insanely great tools for their own enjoyment.

up   Online Jargon   *Adjective*

Functional; available.

updater   Online Jargon   *Noun*

A program that takes the old version of an existing program and adds whichever bits of data to it required to turn it into a more up-to-date version. Most commonly, updaters are free programs released by software companies to fix software problems that were discovered after the product's initial release. Or at least they claim that they didn't know about them. All the ethics of a handful of wet gravel, those software companies. …

upload   Technical Term   *Verb*

To send a file to an online host. *See Also:* **download**

URL   Technical Term   *Noun*

Uniform Resource Locator. A standardized way of defining the address of an Internet resource, which allows your Internet software to determine what sort of resource it is. For instance, the "http" in the URL "http://www.lycos.com/" says it's a webpage; the "mailto" in the URL "mailto:andyi@world.std.com" says it's a place to send e-mail, etc.

Usenet   Online Entity   *Noun*

The Internet Proper's version of a public message base. Usenet consists of thousands of individual newsgroups distributed all over the world, discussing thousands of disparate topics. Usenet is distinct from the public message forums on CompuServe and America Online for two very big reasons. First, it's an enormous beast, several orders of magnitude greater in terms of both users and messages. This means that Usenet can specialize on just about every technical, recreational and social area of discourse imaginable. If you're a mathematician interested in discussing the n6 characteristics of Rolf's Progression with fellow mathematicians (whee!), you can find a "newsgroup" for just such a discussion on Usenet. The second distinction is that Usenet is very much an untamed frontier, and so message topics as well as the messages themselves can get pretty insane. As in "just the names of some of the raunchier newsgroups can cause your jawbone to fuse to your sternum." *See also:* **newsgroup**

userlog   Technical Term   *Noun*

The file on a computer in which the list of people who've used the system, and when, is maintained.

UTC   Technical Term   *Noun*

Universal Time Coordinated. Astonishingly geeky (and official) synonym for Greenwich Mean Time.

.uu   Technical Term   *Noun*

File extension for uuencoded file.

UUCP   Technical Term   *Noun*

Unix to Unix Copy Program. In the dim misty past of the Internet, the standard file-transfer software and mechanisms for moving files around from machine to machine. uucp was used to handle both private mail and support the distribution of Usenet newsgroups.

uuencode   Technical Term   *Noun/Verb*

A UNIX utility that converts a binary file to a text file for the purpose of transmitting it over the Internet. This allows the complicated structure of the original to come through unscathed when handled by the rather unsophisticated systems that handle e-mail and Usenet posts. Almost all of the binary files you find posted on Usenet are there in the form of uuencoded data; any newsreader worth its salt will automatically transmogrify it into its original binary format for you. Because uuencoding is so ubiquitous, most archiving software for Macs and Windows machines can process uuencoded data.

V. Standards   Technical Term   *Noun*

Just as you can't operate a Sony VCR with the

remote control from your Goldstar, two modems manufactured by different companies wouldn't be able to communicate with each other without the existence of formal standards. To make sure that all of the communications gear of the world can get along like one big, happy family, the ITU-T (Inter-national Telecommunication Union-Telecommunication sector; formerly known as the CCITT) was estab-lished to define standards as necessary. With very few excep-tions, a V. standard is one that was defined after a long process of development, comment, and debate.

V.22   Technical Term   *Noun*

The standard for communications at 1,200 bps.

V.22bis   Technical Term   *Noun*

The standard for communications at 2,400 bps.

V.23   Technical Term   *Noun*

A 1,200 bps standard used in Great Britain.

V.32   Technical Term   *Noun*

The standard for 9,600 bps communication, allowing the speed to drop back to 4,800 if the quality of the phone line decreases and then return to 9,600 if it subsequently improves.

V.32bis   Technical Term   *Noun*

V.32 plus connection speeds of 7,200, 12,000, and 14,400 bps. Speed can automatically increase and decrease as the condition of the phone line degrades and improves.

V.32terbo   Technical Term   *Noun*

V.32 plus connection speeds of up to 21.6 Kbps.

V.34   Technical Term   *Noun*

V.32bis with the ability to go as high as 28.8 Kbps.

V.42   Technical Term   *Noun*

A standard for a set of features that allows a modem to automatically detect and correct errors, using the LAPM method.

V.42bis   Technical Term   *Noun*

V.42 plus a scheme for automatic data compression

that can theoretically increase transmission speed by a factor of four.

V.Fast   Technical Term   *Noun*

A proprietary standard for 28.8 Kbps communications, developed by Rockwell when it became clear that the "official" 28.8 standard wouldn't be ratified for quite a while and in the meantime there were tens of thousands of people willing to shell out major bucks for a 28.8 modem.

vaporware   Online Jargon   *Noun*

A product that has been announced but hasn't shipped, especially if it's months and months past its originally announced ship date, e.g., "Apple promised to ship System 8 in 1995, but here it is, late 1996 and it's still vaporware!" Sometimes simply announcing vaporware can act as a preemptive strike—if a huge company like, say, MacroHard announces the impending release of a program that links your coffeepot to an external port on your computer, no one else will bother developing coffeeware 'cause they know MH will squash 'em. For MH to announce this when all they have is the idea would be majorly uncool, and would probably lead a hypothetical corporation like MacroHard to run into trouble with the FTC.

VAX   Technical Term   *Noun*

Virtual Address Extension. A minicomputer that Digital

Equipment Corporation made and then sold everywhere. Very much eclipsed in the Eighties, but worthy
of inclusion here because many old-timers in their mid
to late twenties get misty-eyed when they begin to
discuss the thing.

vbg   Online Style   *Interjection*

See *Instead:* **grin**

Veeb   Online Jargon   *Noun*

See *Instead:* **Veeblefetzer**

Veeblefetzer   Online Jargon   *Noun*

A hapless, miserable, stinking corporate type.

Veronica   Technical Term   *Noun*

A system of servers and protocols on the Net that
allows you to search for information on the worldwide system of Gopher servers. By running a Veronica
client and specifying some topics or keywords,
Veronica will return a list of Gopher sites containing
that info. Obsoleted when Gopher itself was obsoleted by the Web.

vi   Product   *Noun*

Almost comically difficult-to-use text editor for UNIX
systems; unfortunately, often the default editor on
UNIX-based mail and newsreaders. The saints weep,
honestly. You don't see vi around so much because
EMACS is about 179,823.92 times more powerful.

virgin   Online Jargon   *Adjective*

Unused and untainted. Hey, I don't make these things
up! Don't complain to me! When a piece of software
is wonking up, people might recommend that you re-
install it from virgin copies, that is, your master disks.
Because that copy has never actually run, if the re-
installed copy still wonks up you can be sure it's not
because the program files have become tainted.

virus   Technical Term   *Noun*

A piece of software that does with and to computers
what real viruses do to living organisms. When
attached to a "host" program, a virus program installs
itself in memory when the host is run, makes copies
of itself, and infects other programs and/or System
files. This alone can be devastating (all of your computer's time and space are devoted to making copies of
viruses), but viruses can be programmed with other
functions, too, such as wiping out all of your files after
waiting a certain amount of time. Viruses get a lot of
press, but are really of rather minor concern to most

people. You can only become infected by running infected software, which rules out almost all software
you find on commercial online services (which tests all
of its files before they're made public) and almost certainly all commercial software (because the company
which publishes it doesn't want to get sued by 100,000
users). The pedigree of software you download from
the Internet Proper is somewhat more suspect, as it
might not be subject to the same screening process.
But certainly the easiest way to pick up a virus is to
take a disk to a campus computer lab or use it on a
large company network. Countermeasures are readily
available. For every platform "antivirus," programs exist
that can "disinfect" your hard drive and furthermore
innoculate it against known viruses. Because viruses
are a universally feared and hated problem, many such
programs are created and maintained by the Internet
community and released as freeware.

VRML   Technical Term   *Noun*

Virtual Reality Markup Language. An extension of
HTML for the creation of online virtual reality. Will
probably catch on and take the country by storm to
the same extent that those 3-D movie glasses caught
on in the Fifties and never, ever turned out to be just
a brief fad.

WAIS   Technical Term   *Noun*

Wide Area Information Server. An Internet dictionary

of indexes to information, which can be searched with software like Archie and Veronica. Was very much a big deal before the Web came along.

WAN   Technical Term   *Noun*

Wide-Area Network. A network that allows machines far away from each other to communicate, as opposed to a Local Area Network. Technically speaking, the Internet is in itself a WAN, but normally WAN is used to refer to a private network that offers only basic, office-type services. *See Also:* **LAN**

Wap!   Online Jargon   *Interjection*

In online conferencing, the text equivalent of reaching across the table and giving you a deserved whack in the head. A Wap! is more playful than aggressive.

-ware   Online Jargon   *Suffix*

A handy construction which allows you to generate your own jargon and buzzwords. Just imagine a concept which can be expressed in the form "[word] sort of computer-related stuff", replace "sort of computer-related stuff" with "-ware," and you're off and running, as in "pulpware" (the stack of papers on your desk), "cheezware" (Cheez Doodles, Cheez-Its, Goldfish, and related snackware), and "defenestware" (software and hardware of such shoddy design that it's soon thrown out the window).

warez   Online Jargon   *Noun*

Slang for software available for downloading. Often used to specifically refer to pirated software.

Wargames dialer   Online Jargon   *Noun*

A piece of software that dials all phone numbers in a specific exchange, looking for modems. Very obnoxious and also illegal in most parts of the country. Gets its name from the classic film starring Matthew Broderick, in which such a program features prominently.

.WAV   Technical Term   *Noun*

File extension for Windows Waveform soundfile format.

webcast   Online Jargon   *Noun*

To broadcast something live over the World Wide Web. Usually this means hooking up a live-video camera and installing a cgi script that continuously grabs images and sticks them onto your webserver, but the webcast can also involve live text or audio.

webmaster   Online Jargon   *Noun*

Technically speaking, a webmaster is the person who's responsible for the technical needs of a webserver. He or she makes sure that the hardware and software is up and running, that it's secure and that its outside connections are reliable. As a practical matter, however, the term is also applied to the people responsible for the content of a website. Think of a newspaper, which has an editor in chief and a person who's in charge of running the presses. By the "tight" definition, only the pressman is a webmaster, but, under the popular definition, the EIC is, too.

webpage   Technical Term   *Noun*

An individual document on the World Wide Web. As a physical entity, a webpage is a text file on a webserver, a file whose contents have had HTML tags applied to them and can be viewed with a browser program. *See Also:* **website, webserver, HTML**

webserver   Technical Term   *Noun*

A machine on the Internet that acts as a host for a website. A webserver can host more than one website, each of which exists completely independently of the other(s). *See Also:* **website, webpage**

website   Technical Term   *Noun*

A destination on the Web. A website may consist of
any number of individual webpages representing many
topics and many authors, but conceptually all of those
pages are thought of as parts of the larger website.
See Also: **webserver, webpage**

wetware   Online Jargon   *Noun*

The hideously unreliable computing and processing
apparatus, if any, installed between your ears.

Example Look, I just got into the office and
my wetware isn't online yet. Could
you call me back in a couple of hours?

Windows   Technical Term   *Noun*

That which you stare out of forlornly at an unfolding
sunrise, realizing that if you had a Mac, you would have
had your project done twelve hours ago instead of
being forced to spend the entire evening unsuccessful-
ly trying to convince Microsoft Windows that your
laser printer is actually plugged into your printer port
and switched on. There are currently three "flavors" of
Windows in common use: Windows 3.1, the old version which is run by users who can't afford to buy the
new hardware they'd need to run Windows95;
Windows95, the current version, carrying serious
interface enhancements and new features ("Upgrading
from Windows to Windows95 is like upgrading from

Reagan to Bush: It's an improvement, certainly, but nonetheless..."); and Windows NT, a seriously high-powered version optimized for networks and work-groups and favored amongst power users. While W95 was rolled out with tremendous fanfare and marketing muscle behind it, it is the opinion of most Windows analysts that the OS' future lies in Windows NT and not Windows95.

W95   Product   *Noun*

Shorthand for Windows95.

Windoze   Online Jargon   *Noun*

Derisive term for "Microsoft Windows," though some would argue that "Microsoft Windows" is a derisive enough term in its own right.

Winnage   Online Jargon   *Noun*

A winning situation. The opposite of Lossage.

WinSock   Product   *Noun*

Windows Sockets. The Wintel standard API for bringing TCP/IP functionality to Windows. WinSock is a standard created and maintained by Microsoft and other players in the Wintel industry, and several incarnations of WinSock are available from a variety of different sources. You're probably using Trumpet WinSock, which is a strictly freeware version most ISP give away free as part of their sign-up kit.

Wintel   Online Jargon   *Noun*

Windows/Intel. Refers to a computer that runs Microsoft Windows. One of the many problems this hardware creates for the community is one of simple nomenclature. The defining operating system for the thing is Windows, of course, but the hardware itself can be made by any of hundreds of different manufacturers. If you own a Macintosh, you say "I have a Mac," and the listener knows what sort of hardware and software you're interested in. What do Windows users say (besides "Hey, Windows can't find my sound hardware!")? Hence the popularity of this term. "I'm a Wintel guy."

wirehead   Online Jargon   *Noun*

Complimentary term referring to a hacker who's obsessed with knowing everything about electronic hardware or, less frequently, about networks, specifically.

wizard   Online Jargon   *Noun*

One step below net.godhood; an individual who can make the technology do arcane and wonderful things and can be counted on for having the right answers. S/he might not give them to you, but…

wonky   Online Jargon   *Adjective*

(Of hardware or software) unreliable and prone to crash; or with a boatload of quirks which you would rather do without.

workstation   Technical Term   *Noun*

A class of computer used to refer to a machine significantly more powerful (or suited to a specific purpose) than more popular mass-market computers. This distinction has becomed somewhat blurred, however, as performance of desktop computers skyrockets while prices plummet. A typical PowerPC or Pentium machine of today has all of the performance of a fairly exotic graphics workstation of just a few years ago.

World Wide Web   Technical Term   *Noun*

Where the action is. Imagine that your local public library has an enormous loose-leaf binder, and everyone in town is permitted to add pages to it. Anyone, whether they're a parent of three who wants to share a bread recipe or a schoolkid who wants people to see his essay on his life or the local government that wants its legislative decisions to be available, can simply write it out on paper and stick it in the binder. In due time, it becomes thousands of pages thick with contributions from all walks of life on all topics. Oh, and the librarian keeps this book indexed, so if you want to know something about the movie Casablanca, a simple search will turn up the local newspaper's review of the movie, as well as that of a retired movie buff and news that the corner theater will be screening it a week from Thursday. Now expand the concept so that it's not just your town but the entire planet that contributes to this book, and you've got the ongoing international passion play that is the World Wide Web. Websites are accessed via special software called a browser. Give the browser the address (called a URL) of a webpage, and the browser will automatically download all of its text, graphics, and what-have-you and format if for display on your screen. Webpages can contain text, graphics, even sound and video—literally anything that can exist as a file on a computer can be made available in a webpage. "Page" is a bit of a misnomer; an individual "page" can be of any length. A more accurate term would be "Web-document." A collection of such documents is called a website, much like a collection of related writings on a topic would be considered a book.

Let me put it this way: if the Web had been around in the sixties, Sinatra would have been the first one on board. *That's* how hip the Web is.

worm   Technical Term   *Noun*
....

A bit of network nastiness in the same class of evil as the software virus. Worms are network-driven, activating on a computer, looking for other computers the worm can reach, copying itself into those computers, and ordering them to run. Eventually, every single computer that has any sort of connection to that first computer grinds to a halt, doing nothing but sending worms to other computers, and the whole net comes crashing down.

WTF   Online Jargon   *Interjection*

What The Fudge?

WWW   Technical Term   *Noun*

See *Instead:* **World Wide Web**

X Windows   Product   *Noun*

A set of standardized low-level graphics and windowing functions through which UNIX sets up a graphical user interface, such as Motif.

X-10   Technical Term   *Noun*

Extremely way-cool protocol for sending electronic signals through your house's electrical wiring to special control boxes. This allows your computer to control all of the lights and appliances in your home. X-10 geeks tend to be a very freaky lot, but man, if one of them invites you to his or her home, definitely sign up for the whole tour. The Push-Button Home Of The

Future, just like in the old "Daffy Duck" cartoon, I'm
telling ya.

XModem   Technical Term   *Noun*

Ancient and inefficient file-transfer protocol. Has been
extended a number of times: XModem CRC (with
extra—and now useless—error-checking), XModem-
1K (faster), and WXModem (which works faster
under certain conditions…big whoop.) Essentially,
XModem is the protocol of last resort. Almost every
machine supports it, so you can count on it working,
but it's a dramatic step down from any other protocol
you're used to.

XModem Waltz   Online Jargon   *Noun*

A piece of music I composed exclusively while waiting
for files to download. I mention this only because, well,
don't take for granted how great these here modern
high-speed modems are. A nice v.34 modem can
download ten megabytes of data in about an hour. In
the time it took me to download a grand total of ten
megs with my first modem (300 bps), the Xmodem
Waltz had grown to about forty verses and became
slighly longer than the long version of *Alice's Restau-
rant*. It is not nearly as commercial, though, lacking
both the driving beat and the memorable hook needed for Top 40 airplay in today's competitive market.

YA   Online Jargon   *Suffix/Modifier*

Yet Another, usually put at the beginning of another acronym.

Yahoo!   Online Entity   *Noun*

Very popular Internet search engine, found at http://www.yahoo.com/. Popular for its handy topic lists, organized like one really mega-big outline.

YModem   Technical Term   *Noun*

A wildly improved XModem that is far faster and more flexible. Also available in the flavor YModem-G, which is dashed useful in that this flavor does no error-checking whatsoever (like ZModem under the right conditions). If you've got an error-checking modem, YModem-G will probably be the fastest download protocol.

.Z   Technical Term   *Noun*

File extension for uucompressed files.

.ZIP   Technical Term   *Noun*

File extension for ZIP archive file format.

ZModem   Technical Term   *Noun*

The modern and nifty protocol that obsoletes all the
other PC-based protocols. It's faster and more reliable,
plus it adds crash recovery (if your idiot housemate
trips over your modem cord when you were right in
the middle of an hourlong download, ZModem will
wisely just pick up where you left off the next time
you try to download that same file) and the ability to
intelligently choose to let the modem do all the error
checking if it has that protocol.